THE BASILEIA LETTERS
Volume 2

by
Ron McGatlin
(Brother Ron)

"THE BASILEIA LETTERS, Volume 2"
is a compilation of teaching letters written
by Ron McGatlin in the years 1999-2000,
just prior to and at the turn of the
century and the millennium.

THE BASILEIA LETTERS
Volumes 2

Copyright 2001
Ron McGatlin
all rights reserved

ISBN 0-9654546-3-0

All Scripture Quotations Are From the
"New King James Version".
Copyright 1983 by Thomas Nelson, Inc.

Published by
BASILEIA PUBLISHING
107 W. Independence Blvd.
Mt. Airy, NC 27030

http://www.basileiapublishing.com

Printed in the USA by

MORRIS PUBLISHING

3212 East Highway 30 • Kearney, NE 68847 • 1-800-650-7888

Contents

Holiness in the Kingdom of God 4

The Changing Church In The Kingdom of God 17

The Secret Place In The Kingdom of God 30

The Loftiness of Man And The Kingdom of God 43

Renewal And The Kingdom of God 56

Increasing Release of Glory In The Kingdom of God 65

Time of The Kingdom of God 77

Family And The Kingdom of God 86

Change And The Kingdom of God 98

Transformation To The Kingdom of God 107

Power In The Kingdom of God 119

Waiting And Listening For The Kingdom of God 128

Awakening of The Kingdom of God 137

Innocence In The Kingdom of God 146

Pain & Suffering In The Kingdom of God 155

Victory In The Kingdom of God 165

BASILEIA LETTER
Number 13

Holiness in the Kingdom of God

Jesus was called the "holy" Servant of God. *(Acts 4:30)* Many other people, places, and things are referred to as holy in the Bible. Believers are instructed to be holy and live holy lives.

*1 Pet 1:15-16: But as **He who called you is holy, you also be holy in all your conduct,** because it is written, "**Be holy, for I am holy.**"*

What does being holy really mean?

In a practical sense, what is holiness? As believers entering the kingdom emphasis age, what exactly is holiness to us? Are we holy? If not, how can we achieve holiness?

In the passing church emphasis age, different views were taught by theologians regarding holiness and how it could or could not be obtained in the lives of Christians. All of us who have been believers for very long have been taught and trained by one or more of these views. We may be questioning and perhaps changing some of our previously held views. Nevertheless, we each may remain persuaded to some degree by our past training.

In the emerging kingdom emphasis age, fresh light from God continues to confirm the Word of God and wash away many of our past religious views, as it enlightens us to higher kingdom principles.

The reality of holiness now in this life is the kingdom of heaven way.

Some of the past religious views regarding holiness involved externally applied force from religious structures to keep rules, ordinances, forms, and rituals. The religious structures prescribed punishments, (either formally or informally) for lack of adherence to the system of rules and rituals.

Through the centuries many forms and degrees of punishments have been employed. These ranged from death by burning alive at the stake, to mild rejections such as, lack of personal warmth, lack of recognition, lack of acceptance, or loss of privileges. In the minds of some Christians, excommunication from the church threatens their eternal salvation. To others being "kicked out of the church" (sometimes referred to as "the left foot of fellowship") just means going somewhere else to church.

The attempt is to produce holiness in the people by causing them to exert their effort to not do the evil things that they desire in their hearts to do. The fear of being discovered and being publicly or privately punished causes the people to try harder to adhere to the rules and not do the things they really want to do. This is a hard and frustrating life for the people who must always be striving with great effort to not do the evil they really want to do. They may also live in fear that the times they have slipped will be discovered.

In an attempt to achieve holiness, some churches established rules regarding dress, appearance, participation in social activities or entertainment, level of giving to the church, church attendance, and other areas of conduct. These may be presented to the new convert or applicant and a signed agreement required before they are allowed to become a member of the church. Or the church member may be trained in less formal ways to keep religious rules and rituals after joining the church.

The attempt to produce holiness by establishing rules and causing others to keep them is the same approach used by the Pharisees in the early centuries. The Pharisees were generally esteemed to be most holy people, especially among themselves.

Jesus made it clear that this attempt at holiness would not enter the kingdom. The righteousness of trying hard to keep laws, rules, and rituals is not good enough to enter the, now at hand, kingdom of heaven age. Kingdom holiness must exceed even the best attempts to keep religious rules.

Mat 5:20: **For I say to you, that unless your righteousness exceeds the righteousness of the scribes and Pharisees, you will by no means enter the kingdom of heaven.**

Another church age view proffers that we can never live holy lives in the reality of the practical world now. And that we are all sinners and sin every day by continuously coming short of the mark. But that we are positionally holy and righteous before God by faith in the cross of Christ Jesus. Usually, the belief is included that Christians will be able to live in practical holiness after the bodily return of Christ Jesus to defeat the devil and establish His kingdom.

In this view, the Christian is relieved of the responsibility of participating in the defeat of the enemy and the establishing of the kingdom of God on earth now. Also, in this view, practical holiness must wait for the bodily return of Jesus.

Neither of these views from the passing church age are potent to overcome evil and produce practical holiness in this life now. Form, ritual, and religious conformity may feel comfortable and assuring to the participant, but true holiness will not result from forms, rituals, and attempting to conform to religious codes of conduct.

Similarly, the belief that practical holiness is not a viable potential for life today, does not lead to practical holiness now. Believing in only positional righteousness causes a release of responsibility for real and practical holiness now. This also may feel secure and peaceful. Yet, it is dangerous and will not produce true holiness in life now.

Holiness is a matter of the heart and requires a power greater than human effort.

Only the Holy One can produce true kingdom of God holiness. There is only One who is holy and therefore only One who can produce holiness. Jesus said that there is only One who is good.

Mark 10:18: So Jesus said to him, **"Why do you call Me good? No one is good but One, that is, God.**

Jesus lived a perfectly holy life. He and He alone lived a life of true and complete holiness. Jesus did the works that He did by the power of the Holy Spirit. Jesus was led by, and empowered by the Holy Spirit.

Luke 4:1: **Jesus, being filled with the Holy Spirit,** *returned from the Jordan and* **was led by the Spirit** *into the wilderness, .*
Luke 4:14: Then Jesus returned **in the power of the Spirit** *to Galilee, and news of Him went out through all the surrounding region.*

Believers will only walk in holiness by the power of the Holy One, Jesus, bringing forth the power of the One who raised Christ Jesus from the dead, the One who empowered Jesus and the first century apostles, and the One who now empowers believers to live holy powerful lives. The indwelling Spirit of Christ brings redemption which clears the channel for the Spirit of God to flow freely into the believers life, producing true holiness. Power is required to live righteously.
The same power that heals the sick, cast out demons, and preforms miracles is the power that produces holiness.

Rom 15:18-19a: For I will not dare to speak of any of those things which **Christ** *has not* **accomplished through me,** *in word and deed, to make the Gentiles obedient;* **in mighty signs and wonders, by the power of the Spirit of God.**

1 Cor 6:11: And such were some of you. But you were washed, but you were **sanctified,** *but you were justified* **in the name of the Lord Jesus** *and* **by the Spirit of our God.**

Christ Jesus was:
- born of the Holy Spirit,
- led by the Holy Spirit,
- empowered by the Holy Spirit,
- resurrected by the Holy Spirit,
- and now lives in you and me by the Holy Spirit to produce the power of holiness.

Luke 1:35: And the angel answered and said to her, "The **Holy Spirit will come upon you, and the power of the Highest will overshadow you;** *therefore, also,* **that Holy One who is to be born will be called the Son of God.**

Rom 8:9-11: But you are not in the flesh but in the Spirit, if indeed the **Spirit of God dwells in you.** *Now if anyone does not have the* **Spirit of Christ,** *he is not His.*

And if **Christ is in you,** *the body is dead because of sin, but the* **Spirit is life** *because of righteousness.*

But if the Spirit of Him who raised Jesus from the dead dwells in you, He who raised Christ from the dead will also give life to your mortal bodies through His Spirit who dwells in you.

It is the Spirit of Father God who raised Christ Jesus from the dead and now lives in believers to produce His holiness within us.

*Gal 1:1: Paul, an apostle (not from men nor through man, but through **Jesus Christ and God the Father who raised Him from the dead**).*

Holiness and power is only by the grace of God. The Greek word translated "grace" means the work of God within the heart and the outworking of that into the life. Some perverted definitions of grace were prevalent in the church emphasis age which distorted the picture of God living in us to produce true and practical holiness in daily living. Grace was generally seen as a covering for sin rather than a cleansing from sin by the gift of the power of God within.

Grace is cleansing from sin, not just a covering for sin.

The "Strongs Concordance and Greek Dictionary" defines "charis", the Greek word translated "grace", as follows:
G5485. charis, khar'-ece; from G5463; graciousness (as gratifying), of manner or act (abstr. or concr.; lit., fig. or spiritual; espec. **the divine influence upon the heart, and its reflection in the life;** including gratitude):--acceptable, benefit, favour, gift, grace (-ious), joy liberality, pleasure, thank (-s, -worthy).

The powerful presence of God within does not just empower one to not do evil things that one desires in his heart to do.

The Holy Spirit of God washes away the evil desires of the heart.

The brightness of the presence of God melts the darkness of evil desire and causes the will of God to be planted and performed in the purified heart. No longer is there a great striving within to overcome various lusts and evil desires. Evil desires are overcome by the presence of God. Holiness includes freedom from the internal conflict.

Paul spoke of the inner conflict, of which he was delivered by Christ Jesus.

Rom 7:15 KJV: For that which I do I allow not: for what I would, that do I not; but what I hate, that do I.

Rom 7:19-25 KJV: For the good that I would I do not: but the evil which I would not, that I do. Now if I do that I would not, it is no more I that do it, but sin that dwelleth in me. I find then a law, that, when I would do good, evil is present with me. For I delight in the law of God after the inward man: But I see another law in my members, warring against the law of my mind, and bringing me into captivity to the law of sin which is in my members. ***O wretched man that I am! Who shall deliver me from the body of this death? I thank God through Jesus Christ our Lord.***

Paul could not attain victory over the inner conflict of sins of the flesh by trying hard to keep rules or rituals. Yet, he did not remain in subjection to the sinful desires of the flesh. He was not doomed to spend his life on earth in inner strife and conflict, sometimes winning and sometimes loosing the battle with the sins of the flesh.

Deliverance is through Jesus Christ our Lord, by the Holy Spirit.

Gal 5:16-18: I say then: ***Walk in the Spirit, and you shall not fulfill the lust of the flesh.*** *For the flesh lusts against the Spirit, and the Spirit against the flesh; and these are contrary to one another, so that you do not do the things that you wish. But if you are* ***led by the Spirit****, you are not under the law.*

Holiness is produced by the presence of God.

The great outpourings of the presence and power of God, by the Holy Spirit, in the seventh millennium are bringing forth the reality of practical holiness among believers who come to and remain in the powerful presence of God.

Repentance is quick for the believer in the presence of God. **One's sins are never as dark as when seen in the brightness of the light of the presence of God.**

Willingness and agreement are the part of the believer. The presence of the Holy Spirit convicts of sins and is present to cleanse, but a lack of willingness and agreement can prevent the work of the Holy Spirit from bringing holiness.

If one is not willing to come to the place where the presence of God is being poured out by the Holy Spirit, or if one is not willing to agree with God about one's sin, there may be no holiness imparted into the life. If however, there is willingness and agreement there will be impartation of holiness in the powerful presence of God.

Holy living is not something we do.
It is imparted to us by God.

Abraham believed God and gave Him glory. After carrying out God's instruction, righteousness was imputed to Him. Now in the kingdom age it is possible to remain in the presence of God so that life can become an experience of practical holiness; as righteousness is imputed to the believer by the Holy Spirit through Christ in the presence of God.

*Rom 4:20-24: He did not waver at the promise of God through unbelief, but was **strengthened in faith, giving glory to God,** and being fully convinced that what He had promised He was also able to perform.*

*And therefore "it was accounted to him for righteousness." Now it was not written for his sake alone that it was **imputed to him, but also for us. It shall be imputed to us who believe in Him who raised up Jesus our Lord from the dead.***

If Abraham had not believed God and taken the actions prescribed by God, he would not have had righteousness imputed to him. If Christians today refuse to fully trust the one who dwells within them, the One who raised Christ from the dead, and refuse to come to the places where the outpouring of the Holy Spirit is taking place they may fail to have holiness imparted to them. They may not see their sin and repent if they will not come to the places of manifest presence of God coming forth in the outpouring of the Holy Spirit.

The good news (gospel) of the kingdom is brought forth only by the power of the Holy Spirit. A different gospel may be taught or preached by the understanding of man in the power of the soul and intellect of man. (Gal 1:6-12) (2 Cor 11:3) The glorious gospel of the kingdom can only be brought in demonstration of power and words of Christ Jesus by the Holy Spirit.

*Mat 4:23: And Jesus went about all Galilee, teaching in their synagogues, **preaching the gospel of the kingdom**, and **healing all kinds of sickness and all kinds of disease among the people.***

*Mat 10:7-8: And as you go, **preach**, saying, **'The kingdom of heaven is at hand.'** **Heal the sick, cleanse the lepers, raise the dead, cast out demons**. Freely you have received, freely give.*

*Mat 12:28: But if **I cast out demons** by the Spirit of God, **surely the kingdom of God has COME UPON you.***

When the gospel of the kingdom "COMES UPON" believers in power, demons are cast out, sickness is healed, and the dead are raised. The power of the gospel of the kingdom is the source of holiness in believers who have been "come upon" by the kingdom of God.

If there is no demonstration of the power of God, it is not the gospel of the kingdom and there will not be holiness produced. The vast numbers of miracles, healings, people being set free from bondages, the dead being raised, the blind seeing, the deaf hearing, and many giving their lives to God, being reported around the world are the signs that the kingdom of God has come upon us.

The mighty outpouring of the Holy Spirit is bringing renewal and revival as the gospel is being fully preached and demonstrated again on our small planet. Paul and the other apostles brought forth mighty signs and wonders by the power of the Spirit of God, in the first century, as they "fully preached the gospel".

*Rom 15:18-19: For I will not dare to speak of any of those things which **Christ has not accomplished through me, in word and deed**, to make the Gentiles obedient; in **mighty signs and wonders**, by the power of the Spirit of God, so that from Jerusalem and round about to Illyricum **I have fully preached the gospel of Christ**.*

Just as Christ Jesus preached, taught, and demonstrated the gospel of the kingdom two thousand years ago, while in His natural body, He is today preaching, teaching, and powerfully demonstrating the same gospel of the kingdom, while in His earthly spiritual body. The purified believers are the body of Christ on earth. *(1 Cor 12:27)* He again lives within us to bring forth the gospel of the kingdom by the Holy Spirit.

In the church emphasis age incomplete versions of the gospel were preached with different emphasis among different groups. The meaning of the Greek word "euaggelion", translated "gospel" in the new Testament, is simply "a good message".

Strongs Greek Dictionary:

G2098. euaggelion, yoo-ang-ghel'-ee-on; from the same as G2097; **a good message**, i.e. the gospel:--gospel.

A number of "good messages" (gospels) are mentioned in the Scripture. The gospels of the New Testament are different aspects or parts of the great gospel of the kingdom. Jesus preached the gospel of the kingdom, which included the different "good messages" or gospels referred to by the writers of the New Testament. There is only one complete gospel and it is the gospel of the kingdom which includes all of the gospels of Scripture.

There are many references in Scripture to the gospel of Jesus Christ, or the gospel of Christ, or Christ's gospel. There is also mention of the gospel of God, and the gospel of the grace of God. Paul speaks of "my gospel" referring to what he preached. He also spoke of the gospel of salvation and the gospel of peace.

The gospel of being born again is one of the parts of the gospel of the kingdom, which was preached by many in the church age. The first step in coming to God is to be born of the Spirit. That is to give one's life to God and receive the Spirit of Christ. There can be no walk in the kingdom of God lifestyle now, and no hope of heaven after death, for the one who has not been born again.

This is obviously a primary part of the gospel. Yet, it is only a part of the greater gospel of the kingdom, and by itself, does not produce practical holiness in daily living. It is the beginning and the seed for growth into holy living.

The fullness of the gospel of the kingdom must be powerfully preached and demonstrated to produce holy people, living holy lives. As the Holy One lives within and empowers the person to live a holy life, true holiness is manifest into our world. The gospel of the kingdom is changing lives and our world as the great outpouring of the Holy Spirit "comes upon" believers, in renewals and revivals in places around the world.

Holiness is the presence of God.

Holy is defined as "having a **spiritually pure quality, referring to the divine, that which has its sanctity directly from God or is connected with Him**." To seek to be holy means to seek to become soaked or saturated in the presence of God. The baptism of the Holy Spirit means to be soaked, to be completely immersed into the Spirit of God.

*Mark 1:7-8: And he preached, saying, "There comes One after me who is mightier than I, whose sandal strap I am not worthy to stoop down and loose. "I indeed baptized you with water, but **He will baptize you with the Holy Spirit**."*

Mark 16:15-18: And He said to them, "Go into all the world and preach the gospel (the gospel of the kingdom) *to every creature. He who believes and is **baptized*** (baptism of the Holy Spirit, by Jesus) *will be **saved*** (delivered, protected, healed, preserved, made whole); *but he who does not believe will be condemned."*

*"And these **signs** will follow those who believe: In My name they will **cast out demons**; they will **speak with new tongues**; they will **take up serpents**; and if they drink anything deadly, **it will by no means hurt them**; they will **lay hands on the sick**, and they will recover."*

Water baptism is a symbol. Spirit baptism is the powerful reality of being immersed into the Spirit of God. There is no power for holy living, no power for effective ministry to change lives and change the world apart from the baptism into the Spirit of God.

Show me your holiness without the Spirit of God and I will show you your deception, powerlessness, and ineffective religious works.

Show me the awesome manifestations of the power of God, and I will show you the mighty gospel of the kingdom of God, from heaven, being preached and brought forth by the Holy Spirit, to cause the kingdoms of this world to become the kingdoms of our God!

If our ministry is difficult and too hard for us, we are not preaching the gospel of the kingdom in the power of the Holy Spirit. Yes, serious adversity will attempt to overcome us at times. Yet, the awesome power of God will come forth as we continue to believe and faithfully preach the kingdom of God by the power of the Holy Spirit. We must be faithful and obedient to hear and obey the Spirit of God, as He leads us to places of His presence and holiness.

BASILEIA LETTER
Number 14

The Changing Church In The Kingdom of God

Jesus said to the sick man at the pool of Bethesda, **"Do you want to be made well?"** The Greek word translated "well" is "hugies, hoog-ee-ace" and means to be healthy, sound, or whole.

John 5:5-6: Now a certain man was there who had an infirmity thirty-eight years. When Jesus saw him lying there, and knew that he already had been in that condition a long time, He said to him, "Do you want to be made well?"

As I was reading John 5:1-15, God spoke in my spirit and said, "This is a picture of my church without anointing." He caused me to see the church without anointing as a still pool in contrast to the mighty river of the anointed church flowing the power of God by the Holy Spirit.

In the emerging kingdom emphasis age, many churches of the past are being found to be not well, unsound, and in need of wholeness.

As the powerful anointing of Christ brings forth the power of God to save, heal, deliver, and demonstrate the gospel of the kingdom in mighty miracle working power, some impotent churches are being asked the same question that the sick man at the pool of Bethesda was asked, "Do you want to be made well"?

John 5:1-3: After this there was a feast of the Jews, and Jesus went up to Jerusalem. Now there is in Jerusalem by the Sheep Gate a pool, which is called in Hebrew, Bethesda, having five porches. In these lay a great multitude of sick people, blind, lame, paralyzed, waiting for the moving of the water.

Has it not been in the past and does it not continue, that in much of the powerless church, the religious leaders keep the feast of religious ceremonies while a great multitude of sick people lay waiting for the moving of the water?

A multitude of spiritually and physically blind, lame, and paralyzed people fill some churches. Many Christians are in desperate need of the reality of the power of God to heal them and make them sound, well, and whole, to form them into powerful men and women of God, free of the infirmities caused by sin and religion.

The still pool is referred to as "by the sheep gate" in the NKJV and "by the sheep market" in the KJV. These phrases are translated from the Greek word "probatikos, prob-at-ik-os", and means "relating to sheep". Apparently this pool relates to the merchandising of sheep.

Throughout the ages, some religious leaders have made merchandise of God's sheep. Shepherds that should have been feeding and healing the sheep have often fed themselves and failed to bring the river of healing and strengthening to the needy sheep.

Men with power and position of religious structure have often used and abused the sheep. Those who should be strengthened with spiritual food and healed with the power of faith in God, have often been left by the pool while the leaders and religious people feasted at religious ceremonies.

Ezek 34:2-4: Son of man, prophesy against the shepherds of Israel, prophesy and say to them, "Thus says the Lord GOD to the shepherds: Woe to the shepherds of Israel who feed themselves! Should not the shepherds feed the flocks?"

"You eat the fat and clothe yourselves with the wool; you slaughter the fatlings, but you do not feed the flock."
"The weak you have not strengthened, nor have you healed those who were sick, nor bound up the broken, nor brought back what was driven away, nor sought what was lost; but with force and cruelty you have ruled them."

Five porches had been built around the pool of still water, in which only occasionally there was a little movement of the water and someone was healed. Probably, only one porch was initially built and as the multitude of needy people increased, others were built. Have we not built great buildings around a pool of very little power and only an occasional stirring of the water, in the past church age?

I don't know what the porches at Bethesda looked like, but according to the definitions of the Greek wording, they may have had columns of stone supporting a roof. This was a substantial structure that provided for the sick to come each day and lay to wait for the moving of the water or wait to die. Probably, many died and were carried away from the porches to be buried. Is it not true that many have suffered needlessly and died prematurely on our grand porches around our powerless pools?

Whether we like to admit it or not this is a part of the heritage of the church that goes back to the medieval church of the dark ages. Is it possible that some of these ways and patterns have found a hidden place in us? Is it possible that we may have a wrong focus through a heritage of religion and erroneous training? Are we perhaps more concerned with our personal well being and church position than we think we are?

Is it possible that we might not be quick to do anything that might harm our reputation in the arena of church politics?

Is it possible that some of us may have become locked into the doctrines of powerlessness from the still pool of religion and are not aware of it?

The question is to us as it was to the man who had an infirmity for a long time, **"Do you want to be made well"?**

Are we willing to cast off the systems of man made doctrines and religion from the past to take a chance on moving into rivers of flowing, rushing, living water? Are we willing to take a chance on displeasing the ones over us in our religious structure by departing from the traditional still pool of religious theology?

John 5:7: The sick man answered Him, "Sir, I have no man to put me into the pool when the water is stirred up; but while I am coming, another steps down before me."

"I HAVE NO MAN", was the answer to the question. Are not the multitudes of sick sheep around the world crying out today for a man --- a man that will come upon their pitiful scene of sick people on grand porches around powerless pools and do something about it?

God is looking for a man to rise upon the earth -- a man who will make a difference. Jesus Christ is that man. When Jesus showed up at the pool of Bethesda everything began to change.

Today when Jesus shows up and the mighty presence of God is brought forth by the Holy Spirit everything changes. The spiritually and physically sick and afflicted meet the mighty river of God and are healed, set free, and empowered to live holy lives.

God has His Man and He is brought forth from a woman -- the wife of God. It is the purified holy Bride of Christ who is collectively becoming the Body of Christ, the manifestation of Christ Jesus into the world to change the church and the world -- to bring forth the rule and dominion of God -- the kingdom of God on earth.

Jesus Christ in His universal body on earth will stand and speak with power just as He did to the sick man at the pool, "Arise, and pick up your bed off the porch by the powerless pool and walk"---walk in spiritual power and health in the anointing of God.

Have we made our bed on the grand porches by the powerless pool of religion without the movement and flow of the Spirit of God? It is now time for us to meet the power of God and be made whole, and then pick up our bed and walk---walk to the river of God.

John 5:8-9: Jesus said to him, "Rise, take up your bed and walk." And immediately the man was made well, took up his bed, and walked. And that day was the Sabbath.

"Do you want to be made well"? At first glance it seems the answer to this question would be obvious. Who would not want to be made well? Yet, as we read further we realize there may be a price to be paid after being made well. The religious structure is not always pleased when Jesus shows up and miracles take place. Certainly it is difficult for them to find fault with the sick being healed. It is easier to find fault and make a big issue of how or when it was done.

Great revivals of the past have been squelched by religious leaders arguing over doctrines, forms, and practices. Today mighty outpourings of God are producing multitudes of people giving their lives to God, miraculous healings, and deliverance from every form of bondage.

Yet, these outpourings and those working in them are highly criticized by some in the religious community. Like the Jews who criticized the man who was cured, they can only accuse those involved of not doing it the right way.

John 5:10-12: The Jews therefore said to him who was cured, "It is the Sabbath; it is not lawful for you to carry your bed." He answered them, "He who made me well said to me, 'Take up your bed and walk.'" Then they asked him, "Who is the Man who said to you, 'Take up your bed and walk'?"

One possible reason for not wanting to be made well is that it may cost loss of favor with those who remain at the still pool. Another reason might be that some do not know how sick they are. The enemy wants us to believe that what we have is all there is for us. He does not want us to know of the river of God flowing from the throne of God.

Rivers of living water of the Spirit of God are flowing into our world from the hearts of purified believers. The anointing of the anointed one (Christ Jesus) within believers is flowing the life, love, and power of God by His Spirit into the changing church. A corporate anointing of Christ is present as unified believers come together in praise, prayer, and worship.

*John 7:38 -39a: "He who believes in Me, as the Scripture has said, **out of his heart will flow rivers of living water.**" But this He spoke concerning the Spirit, whom those believing in Him would receive.*

*Psa 36:7-9: How precious is Your lovingkindness, O God! Therefore the children of men put their trust under the shadow of Your wings. They are abundantly satisfied with the fullness of Your house, **And You give them drink from the river of Your pleasures. For with You is the fountain of life**; In Your light we see light.*

Rev 22:1: And he showed me a pure river of water of life, clear as crystal, proceeding from the throne of God and of the Lamb.

Jesus spoke of the living water in the conversation with the woman at the well. He spoke these words to her, "If you knew the gift of God". If religious men today knew the gift of God, the powerful water of life of the Spirit, and who Jesus is by the Spirit in His body today, they would surely want to be made well.

*John 4:10-14: Jesus answered and said to her, "**If you knew the gift of God**, and who it is who says to you, 'Give Me a drink,' you would have asked Him, and He would have given you living water."*

*"Whoever drinks of this water will thirst again, but whoever drinks of the water that I shall give him will never thirst. **But the water that I shall give him will become in him a fountain of water springing up into everlasting life**."*

The flow of the river of life of the Spirit of God flowing from individuals together in unity combines to produce the mighty river of spiritual power and anointing that is changing individuals, churches, and our world.

In the passing church age a few "mighty men of God" were expected to flow the river of life for the multitudes. In the emerging kingdom age it is the power of the Spirit of God flowing through all of His people.

Not only were the sheep merchandised in past centuries but in more recent times the gifts of the Spirit have also been merchandised. Gifted men used their gifts to establish profitable ministries and positions.

When Jesus shows up things are different. Notice that after he cured the sick man He simply withdrew into the multitude. He did not attempt to gain anything from the working of the miracles. It was important that he give the healed man a final message so he looked him up later and gave him this important instruction for his life: *"Sin no more, lest a worse thing come upon you."*

John 5:13-14: But the one who was healed did not know who it was, for Jesus had withdrawn, a multitude being in that place. Afterward Jesus found him in the temple, and said to him, "See, you have been made well. Sin no more, lest a worse thing come upon you."

In another passage Jesus said the temple was to be a house of prayer but merchandisers had made it a den of thieves. Probably all of us have either preached or heard good sermons on the cleansing of the temple. And probably inwardly shouted a cheer for Jesus as we imagined Him disrupting the work of the merchandisers and expelling them from the temple.

Is it possible that while we cheered the work of Jesus, we ourselves have been subversively exposed to a system of practices that may have infected us to some degree with the perverted practices of the merchandisers without realizing it?

Is it possible that the increased presence of God coming forth in the temple of our lives and our churches is exposing deeply ingrained practices that may be tainted with the merchandising practices of the past?

Is it time for us to allow the increased light of the presence of God coming forth today, to brightly illumine and search our motives and methods? Or should we continue to reproduce the practices and patterns of the passing age into the emerging kingdom age?

It is time for change, just as it was time for change when Jesus arrived at the temple in Jerusalem. Obviously, Jesus had been there before. Surely, he had seen the tables of the merchandisers before. Yet, He had done nothing about them.

Why was this day the time for Him to take action against a long existing perversion in the house of God? What set the stage for the Son of God to come forth in power and bring powerful correction to the house of God on this day?

The worship and praise of the people released the power of the Lord.

Never before had palm branches and clothing been laid before him. Never before had He been received by the multitudes as "He who comes in the name of the Lord." Never before had acts of worship and shouts of praise for Jesus moved the entire city. Never before had Jesus been given the authority of the people to make these changes in the house of God. **Isn't this a lot like today? It Is Time!**

Today multitudes are worshiping and shouting out praises to God as the presence of God comes forth in the very midst of congregations around the world. The powerful presence of the Holy Spirit is bringing forth the awesome presence of the Lord in power to change us, to change our church, our city, and eventually our world.

Mat 21:8-13: And a very great multitude spread their clothes on the road; others cut down branches from the trees and spread them on the road. Then the multitudes who went before and those who followed cried out, saying: "Hosanna to the Son of David! Blessed is He who comes in the name of the LORD! Hosanna in the highest!" And when He had come into Jerusalem, all the city was moved, saying, "Who is this?" So the multitudes said, "This is Jesus, the prophet from Nazareth of Galilee."

Then Jesus went into the temple of God and drove out all those who bought and sold in the temple, and overturned the tables of the money changers and the seats of those who sold doves. And He said to them, "It is written, 'My house shall be called a house of prayer,' but you have made it a 'den of thieves.'"

The charismatic movement of the recent past came forth in the latter years of the church age emphasis of great mercy. Centuries of "still pool" religion began closing and a new season of stirring of the water began with a great move of spiritual gifts released upon ministers and congregations.

During the charismatic movement, the gifts of God without repentance were poured out upon flesh. The Holy Spirit was sometimes poured out upon spiritual children (those without maturity). Great miracles of healing, prophesy, words of knowledge, and even words of wisdom came forth from spiritually immature men and women.

Many of the gifted yet immature Christians became leaders who set the patterns of practice for the church. These patterns sometimes included merchandising the gifts and many became wealthy through selling the gifts of God.

Please do not miss understand what I am saying. God is not against our prosperity and purity in every area of life. Always having enough to complete God's plans for us is the kingdom way. Things will be added as we seek the kingdom of God and His righteousness first. Yet, did not Jesus say, "Freely you have received, freely give"?

Mat 10:8: Heal the sick, cleanse the lepers, raise the dead, cast out demons. **Freely you have received, freely give.**

New patterns--- kingdom of God patterns of maturity and purity are coming forth today. The stirring of the water of the charismatic error was great, but the mighty river of God that will change our world must flow through clean vessels. As people of God reach spiritual maturity and die to their self ways, the Spirit of Christ the King is manifesting through the Spirit of Him who raised Christ Jesus from the dead. (Rom 8:11)

The Spirit of the resurrected Christ is overtaking our religion and bringing forth the river of God to wash away our defilement and bring life giving nourishment and healing to God's people. The church is now becoming less "churchy", and much more alive.

It is time for the glorious Christ to be formed in His glorified Body on earth. **We are only beginning to experience what it really means to be the Body of Christ on earth.**

We may need to consider our ways. Is it possible that to some degree we have merchandised God's goods--- sold ourselves first, then the gifts He has given us, and the people he has given to us?

Is this possibly the reason our "still pool" is not moving? Is the church spiritually languishing while we take care of our own houses? Have we perhaps worked hard but with a mixed motive and reaped very little spiritual movement as a result?

Hag 1:4-8: "Is it time for you yourselves to dwell in your paneled houses, and this temple to lie in ruins?" Now therefore, thus says the LORD of hosts: "Consider your ways!"

"You have sown much, and bring in little; You eat, but do not have enough; You drink, but you are not filled with drink; You clothe yourselves, but no one is warm; And he who earns wages, Earns wages to put into a bag with holes." Thus says the LORD of hosts: "Consider your ways!"

"Go up to the mountains and bring wood and build the temple, that I may take pleasure in it and be glorified," says the LORD.

After answering the question "Do you want to be made well?" with an absolute, and unqualified YES, we must go up to the mountains--- to the high places with God. We must look up--- look higher to the mountains from which our help comes. Only on the spiritual mountain of God will we find the material to build the temple of God in which He will take pleasure and be glorified. *(Isa 2:3, Micah 4:2, Heb12:22-25)*

Psa 121:1: I will lift up my eyes to the hills; From whence comes my help?

Only clean hands and a pure heart can come to the high places of God and stand in His holy place of ministering the river of the Spirit of God's miracle working power to cleanse, heal, deliver, and make whole.

Psa 24:3-4a: Who may ascend into the hill of the LORD? Or who may stand in His holy place? He who has clean hands and a pure heart...

In a very practical sense we must draw nearer to God and He will draw near to us. Our focus must change from religious systems and trying to meet needs, to intimate worship and communion with Christ.

We can never cause the river to flow from us by trying to make it flow. The flow of the Spirit of God cannot be pumped, it must spring up from God Himself. We must come to Him without the religious framework of the past and seek Him with our whole heart at any and all cost.

James 4:8: Draw near to God and He will draw near to you. Cleanse your hands, you sinners; and purify your hearts, you double-minded.

It is once again time to press in--- time to press into God--- taking our eyes off everything else until we are with Him in the fullness of His presence. It is time to come together and praise Him full out--- worship Him with all we have--- and pray fervently. It is time to call upon Him for the outpouring of living water to flow upon us and from us--- time to cry out for the river of God to flood our families, churches, and cities with His glory.

The river of God flows from the combined water springing up from many hearts. All those gathered together must be in unity of the Spirit. All the disciples gathered in the upper room at Pentecost were in one accord when the mighty rushing wind of the Spirit of God came from heaven upon them. *(Acts 2:1-2)*

All the people marched around Jericho together in complete silence until the appointed time and then they all shouted together at one time *(Josh 6)*. The whole world was not in unity but all who were present were in one accord.

We will not enter into the river of God as a group until all present are in one accord. There will in no wise enter in anything that defiles. (Rev 21:27) The New Jerusalem -- the purified Bride of Christ will not be entered by those in discord with the Spirit and flow of God.

Only as all present put their focus on the Lord and seek Him with their whole heart can we come into unity. We cannot focus on religion, doctrine, or worldly things and move into unity. We must focus on Christ and in the power of the Spirit, seek His presence.

We are changed in His presence.

BASILEIA LETTER
Number 15

The Secret Place In The Kingdom of God

*Psa 91:1: He who dwells in the **secret place** of the Most High Shall abide under the shadow of the Almighty.*

The word translated *"secret place"* is the Hebrew word "cether" (say'-ther) and has the meaning of a covering, covert, disguise, private, secret, protection, hiding place. It is almost always translated "hide" or "hid".

Where is the *secret place*? What does the *secret place* mean to me?

Today in some parts of our world, Christians are persecuted and martyred for their faith. In addition to persecution Christians are attacked by sickness and disease. It is very obvious to anyone with open eyes that there are severe problems encountered by many servants of the Lord. Is there really a *secret place* of protection under the shadow of the Almighty--- a refuge from the disorders of our world?

The first century apostles endured severe persecution. Were they unable to find the *secret place*, and therefore persecuted and martyred? Did they in some way miss Psalm 91 and its promises of protection under the shadow of the Almighty? I don't think so!

Obviously the *secret place* is not in a certain geographic location. Indeed, there are places where Christians can find refuge from persecution, but the *secret place* will not be found in a specific geographic location. **The *secret place* is in the Lord.** We can be sheltered and protected in the Lord.

*Psa 91:1-9: He who dwells in the **secret place** of the Most High Shall abide under the shadow of the Almighty.*

I will say of the LORD, "He is my refuge and my fortress; My God, in Him I will trust."

Surely He shall deliver you from the snare of the fowler And from the perilous pestilence.

He shall cover you with His feathers, And under His wings you shall take refuge; His truth shall be your shield and buckler.

***You shall not be afraid** of the terror by night, Nor of the arrow that flies by day, Nor of the pestilence that walks in darkness, Nor of the destruction that lays waste at noonday.*

*A thousand may fall at your side, And ten thousand at your right hand; But it shall not come near you. Only with your eyes shall you look, And see the **reward of the wicked**.*

***Because you have made the LORD**, who is my refuge, Even the Most High, **your dwelling place**.*

Obviously there are many questions and many facets to the answers to these questions. Yet the Word of God is true and Jesus (the Word from God) is truth. (John *1*) He is the way, the truth, and the life. (*John 14:6*) The Word was made flesh and is yet being made flesh as the indwelling Spirit of Christ lives in believers by the Holy Spirit.

Yet, there continues to be great warfare in the world for the souls of mankind. There is yet a generous abundance of sinful and prideful people in our world, including some who claim to be Christians. Where there is sin and pride there is a lack of faith, understanding, and victory in life.

Mankind is still very much in a process of finding out who we are in Christ Jesus. Therefore, much sin, sickness, disease, and premature death is prevalent in our world. Even many who try to do all they know, live in lack of victory. Christians who do not know who they really are in Christ--- who do not know what He has done, and is doing, to bring the overcoming kingdom of God lifestyle into their lives will experience a lack of victory. They do not know how to appropriate the work of Christ into their own lives, nor how to warfare for others.

Knowledge of who we are in Christ will be revealed in the *secret place* of intimacy with our Lord. Victory over every circumstance in life is only possible as we come into intimacy with Christ. Only in His close presence with our ear pressed to His chest can we hear His heart beat and receive ultimate knowledge from Him. However, if there is impurity in our hearts and lives, our iniquity will prevent us from coming into the *secret place* of intimacy, and rob us of victory.

Rom 10:2: For I bear them witness that they have a zeal for God, but not according to **knowledge**.

Job 36:8-12: And if they are bound in fetters, **Held in the cords of affliction,** *Then He tells them* **their work and their transgressions;** *That they have* **acted defiantly**. *He also opens their ear to instruction, And commands that they* **turn from iniquity**.

If they obey and serve Him, They shall spend their days in prosperity, And their years in pleasures. But if they do not obey, They shall perish by the sword, **And they shall die without knowledge**.

Sin is at the core of all sickness, disease, and premature death in our world. **This is not to say that every individual person who is afflicted or persecuted is to blame for their own situation. It is a much bigger and more complex picture than that .** Sin entered through Adam and passed to all mankind. Had there been no sin there would have been no sickness, no disease, and no death. Jesus came to redeem mankind and our world from sin and the curse of sin. *(Rom 5:12-19)*

The knowledge of Christ and who we really are in Him can only be imparted by the Spirit. Only in the presence of God can we come to the realization of the awesome work and power of God available to redeem our world. We must come into the *secret place* of **intimate communion** with God to find the hiding place of protection and the power for victory to overcome evil in our world. We must **KNOW** Him in a deeper greater more intimate way than our past religion has taught us.

To bear the fruit of overcoming and living victoriously in the world we must intimately, closely, and continuously abide in Him. Our dwelling place must be with Him. Psalm 91:1, did not say whoever **visits** the secret place of the most high shall abide in the shadow (protection) of the Almighty. Jesus did not say whoever **visits** me occasionally, or even often, will bear the fruit of a victorious life.

Jesus said, *John 15:4:* *"**Abide in Me, and I in you.** As the branch cannot bear fruit of itself, unless it abides in the vine, neither can you, unless you **abide in Me**.*

John 15:5: "I am the vine, you are the branches. ***He who abides in Me, and I in him****, bears much fruit; for without Me you can do nothing.*

*John 15:11: "These things I have spoken to you, that **My joy may remain in you, and that your joy may be full.***

It is God's plan for His children to walk in full joy. It is His desire that the joy of the Lord remain in us through our abiding in Christ Jesus and He in us. The joy of the Lord in us does not depend on our circumstances.

Our joy depends on the presence of Christ within us by the Holy Spirit.

Psa 31:19 Oh, how great is Your goodness, Which You have laid up for those who fear You, Which You have prepared for those who trust in You In the presence of the sons of men!
Psa 31:20 ***You shall hide them in the secret place of Your presence*** *From the plots of man; You shall keep them secretly in a pavilion From the strife of tongues.*

This may not make sense to our understanding of our circumstances. The presence and peace of God goes beyond the things of circumstances and understanding.

Phil 4:6-9: Be anxious for nothing, but in everything by prayer and supplication, ***with thanksgiving****, let your requests be made known to God;* ***and the peace of God, which surpasses all understanding, will guard your hearts and minds through Christ Jesus.***
Finally, brethren, whatever things are true, whatever things are noble, whatever things are just, whatever things are pure, whatever things are lovely, whatever things are of good report, if there is any virtue and if there is anything praiseworthy; ***meditate on these things****.*
The things which you ***learned*** *and* ***received*** *and heard and saw in me, these do, and the* ***God of peace will be with you.***

Paul knew how to abide in the *secret place* of peace in God whether circumstances seemed uplifting or whether things seemed downcast. He had learned to remain in that *secret place* when he was stoned and run out of town by the religious crowd, or when many were coming to the Lord and miracles were flowing through his ministry. Whether he was in warm fellowship with close friends, or was in a cold prison, he could know the presence and peace of God.

*Phil 4:11-13: Not that I speak in regard to need, **for I have learned in whatever state I am, to be content:** I know how to be abased, and I know how to abound. **Everywhere and in all things I have learned both to be full and to be hungry, both to abound and to suffer need. I can do all things through Christ who strengthens me**.*

Personal well being is not the first priority of servants of God. Paul and every mature disciple of Christ, every sent one of God, knows that they are here to make a difference. We are sent to bring change in our world through Christ. First in the hearts of people and then our world.

As individuals multiply into multitudes walking in the Spirit and meditating the things of God, conditions and circumstances are changed in our world. The time in which we live is a time of major transition from the ways of fallen man ruling our world to the ways of God.

The transition began two thousand years ago as Christ Jesus proclaimed the kingdom of God way of life. Jesus paid the price for redemption of mankind and our world. And afterward, ascended to the right hand of the Father. The early apostles of the Lamb were then kept by the Comforter, the Helper, the Holy Spirit.

They were able to find the peace and protection of the *secret place* in the presence of God by the Holy Spirit. They brought forth and planted the seeds of the kingdom of God which have sprouted and grown through the years. We are partakers of the maturing growth of the kingdom of God.

Obviously, there has been many ups and downs. It has not been and will not be a smooth transition. Resistance from ungodly people, both heathen and religious, inflamed by the evil one who desires his kingdom to rule the earth, has brought many adverse and detrimental circumstances upon the people of God. While the transition is taking place there is a *secret place* of protection for the soul of those who continue to be used of God to bring forth His kingdom.

As kingdom warriors, we will be persecuted, and as many before us we may suffer and pay the supreme price --- the loss of our lives. Yet, we will never be touched by the devastating fear and destructive plagues of the enemy. We may pass from this life. We may be a casualty in the war. Yet, **we will never die.** We will only pass from LIFE unto LIFE. Whether we live or die we shall forever be in the presence of the Lord. (Rom 14:8) (2 Cor 5:8) In the *secret place*, we will live in victory over all fear of pestilence and destruction now. And when we pass from this life, we shall forever remain with Him in the *secret place* of His presence.

Psa 91:5-9 ***You shall not be afraid*** *of the* ***terror*** *by night, Nor of the* ***arrow*** *that flies by day, Nor of the* ***pestilence*** *that walks in darkness, Nor of the* ***destruction*** *that lays waste at noonday. A thousand may fall at your side, And ten thousand at your right hand;* ***But it shall not come near you.*** *Only with your eyes shall you look, And see the* ***reward of the wicked.*** ***Because you have made the LORD****, who is my refuge, Even the Most High,* ***your dwelling place.***

There is more in the *secret place* **than peace and protection. In the secret place we receive impartation and instruction from God.**

Psa 32:7 You are my hiding place; You shall preserve me from trouble; You shall surround me with songs of deliverance. Selah
Psa 32:8 ***I will instruct you and teach you in the way you should go****; I will guide you with My eye.*

Yes, there is comfort and peace apart from our circumstances now. But there is more.--- Direction and power are released by the Holy Spirit to carry out our part in bringing forth the kingdom of God in our world.--- **His power and knowledge are changing our circumstances**.

The circumstances of our world are changing. The great men of faith of the past have not given their lives in vain. We have not given our lives in vain. We have become a part of the chain of people of God bringing forth the kingdom of God in the world. The awesome **love** of God shall rule the world as it rules our lives from within. The kingdoms of this world are becoming the kingdoms of our God as love empowers people of God to give their lives that others may come to the kingdom of God lifestyle in this life.

John 15:12-13: "This is My commandment, that you love one another as I have loved you. "Greater love has no one than this, than to lay down one's life for his friends.

Jesus clearly warned His disciples of the things they would face as He went to the Father. He also told them it was best that He leave them because the great "parakletos"(par-ak'-lay-tos) "intercessor, consoler:--advocate, comforter" would not come until He went to the Father.

John 15:26-27: "But when the Helper comes, whom I shall send to you from the Father, the Spirit of truth who proceeds from the Father, He will testify of Me. And you also will bear witness, because you have been with Me from the beginning."

John 16:1-7: "These things I have spoken to you, that you should not be made to stumble. "They will put you out of the synagogues; yes, the time is coming that whoever kills you will think that he offers God service. "And these things they will do to you because they have not known the Father nor Me."

"But these things I have told you, that when the time comes, you may remember that I told you of them. And these things I did not say to you at the beginning, because I was with you. "But now I go away to Him who sent Me, and none of you asks Me, 'Where are You going?' "But because I have said these things to you, sorrow has filled your heart."

*"Nevertheless I tell you the truth. It is to **your advantage** that I go away; for if I do not go away, the Helper will not come to you; but if I depart, I will send Him to you."*

It was a wonderful thing for the disciples to be with Jesus when He was here on earth in His natural body. It was not easy for the disciples to see Him go back to the Father. Yet, Jesus said it would be better for them than before. It was to their advantage for Him to go.

Today many long for His presence and think of how wonderful it will be when He bodily returns. Christians sometimes feel that something is missing, that there are things that cannot be fulfilled, victories that cannot be won until He bodily returns. Many wish they could have been there and walked with Him when He was here in His natural body.

We must come to the realization that what we have now is **better** than what the disciples had when they walked with Jesus in His natural body. There is nothing missing on God's part. Everything is in place to bring about the will of the Father, the kingdom of God now. There is nothing lacking on God's part to overcome the enemy and destroy His reign upon the earth.

Christ returned to the first century disciples in the Holy Spirit. They were **endued with power from on High** as the Helper mightily descended upon those who were waiting in the place instructed by the Lord. (Luke 24:49) (Acts 2) The power of God that flowed through Jesus before His ascension then came upon the disciples of Christ. They were changed from observers to **doers of the mighty works of God** to bring change.

Supernaturally God took up residence in the hearts of His people. (1 Cor 3:16) Holy Spirit is God just as much as Jesus or the Father are God. We have only one God manifest in three persons. (Mark 12:29) All of the attributes of the Father and the Son flow through the Holy Spirit. Our Helper is the most powerful, most loving, most wise, most knowledgable of all that exist. There is nothing beyond Him. He is the creator and the One who sustains all that exist. He is above all. All creation is subject to Him.

Jesus said, I and my Father are one. (John 10:30) And He said, **We** will make our home with those who love Me. (Rom 8:9-11) (Col 1:27)

*John 14:17-20: ...the Spirit of truth, whom the world cannot receive, because it neither sees Him nor knows Him; but you know Him, for **He dwells with you and will be in you**.*

*I will not leave you orphans; **I will come to you**.*

*A little while longer and the world will see Me no more, but you will see Me. **Because I live, you will live** also.*

*At that day you will know that **I am in My Father, and you in Me, and I in you**.*

*John 14:23 Jesus answered and said to him, "If anyone loves Me, he will keep My word; and My Father will love him, and **We will come to him and make Our home with him**."*

We can meet with God and walk with Him in the *secret place* as we dwell together with God, NOW.

Christians today often rush about working and ministering seeking to do good. Putting out fires of difficulties of every nature in the lives of others. Seeking to bring the work or word to help suffering people and to bring correction to the rebellious.

Much activity is generated seeking to meet the needs of others. Additional jobs are taken on and extra hours of work put in to try to get things needed for the family. For many it seems difficult to search for the *secret place* amidst all there is to be done.

Yet, the answers we need, the power and guidance that will unlock the resources of heaven to overcome every situation of life, will only be found in the *secret place*. We must meet the Almighty and have His direction and empowerment before seeking to deal with the needs of our world. We must spend time close to Him, if we are going to be anointed (rubbed on) by Him.

Jesus went from one isolated place of prayer and communion with God to another, and released awesome miracles to meet the needs of people in between. Jesus today in us will do the same as He did in His natural body.

The world will not be changed--- the kingdom of God will not be established--- by our running around trying to put our fires. **The fires of hell will be quenched in the lives of believers as we find the *secret place* of power and guidance of God.**

We must find our *secret place* with Him. The first priority of disciples of Christ must be to love God with our whole heart. Only a hypocrite could say they love someone with all they have and yet not spend time in intimacy with the one they profess to love.

The *secret place* is that space in which all the world grows dim and leaves our awareness as we intimately bask in His embrace of love and glory. The comfort of the Holy Spirit in His embrace is awesome and complete. We are totally comforted no matter what our circumstances.

Our whole reason for being becomes to express our love for Him--- to worship Him with deep all consuming love. Our mouths and lives are filled with praise for Him as we exceedingly and amorously admire His glory. Our hearts are melted as He pours the liquid fire of His love upon us.

This out pouring of His love brings a great desire to obey Him--- to serve Him at all cost. The greatest desire of our heart is to please Him--- our only fear is that of disappointing Him. We are motivated to whole heartedly serve Him and carefully obey Him.

The empowerment and wisdom imparted to us in the *secret place* of intimacy with Him will enable us to change the world. Great creative ideas and solutions to unsolvable problems can be imparted into our hearts and understanding. Supernatural powers begin to work to change natural circumstances to cause them to come into alignment with the will of God and the job He has given us to do. Miracles are just God working in ways we cannot explain. Nothing is impossible to the one who believes. (Mark 9:23) And the one in intimate love with God will believe in Him without reservation and limitation.

There remains a season of great beauty as the powerful presence of God changes the people of God and our world. Eventually the perilous persecution will give way to a time when God's people will live in a world filled with the peace of God. All who have escaped with their lives through the time of transition and judgment will be holy--- cleansed of the Lord. The kingdom of God coming forth in our world is worth all the cost.

Isa 4:2-6: In that day the Branch of the LORD shall be beautiful and glorious; And the fruit of the earth shall be excellent and appealing For those of Israel who have escaped.

BASILEIA LETTER
Number 15

And it shall come to pass that he who is left in Zion and remains in Jerusalem will be called holy; everyone who is recorded among the living in Jerusalem. When the Lord has washed away the filth of the daughters of Zion, and purged the blood of Jerusalem from her midst, by the spirit of judgment and by the spirit of burning,

Then the LORD will create above every dwelling place of Mount Zion, and above her assemblies, a cloud and smoke by day and the shining of a flaming fire by night. For over all the glory there will be a covering. And there will be a tabernacle for shade in the daytime from the heat, for a place of refuge, and for a shelter from storm and rain.

BASILEIA LETTER
Number 16

The Loftiness of Man And The Kingdom of God

Have you ever experienced the serenity of walking in a beautiful forest of majestic tall trees on a warm sunny day? There is a feeling of security and comfort in the cool shade of the huge trees. One feels at ease and protected by the canopy of giant branches meshing together far overhead. You tend to feel small in the presence of the giant trees, and may have a worshipful respect for the magnificent, stately, ancient trees.

This is how I felt as God recently spoke to me in a powerful prophetic dream. I walked about in the most beautiful oak forest I have ever seen. The trees were huge and over one hundred feet tall. They had magnificent limbs growing this way and that, forming unique patterns high in the trees. The tree trunks were very large and covered with distinctive rough oak bark. The trees were some distance apart but they were so large that they all entwined together forming a beautiful green canopy high overhead.

Beneath the trees, the floor of the forest was open and free of brush. There were no pesky briars or thorny berry vines, no small growth to make walking difficult. I strolled about with ease admiring the awesomeness of the giant magnificent trees. I felt they must be hundreds of years old. There was a sense of strength and personal protection realizing they had stood against the elements with no apparent damage for centuries. Though I could catch small glimpses of bright sun light through the canopy it was wonderfully shady and comfortably cool. There was no concern for heat or sunburn in such a protected environment. It seemed it would be a good place to remain forever and enjoy its comfort and protection.

BASILEIA LETTER
Number 16

    I was well into the forest when I stopped short. The sound of a rushing strong wind came to my ears. Instantly I looked up toward the north from which the sound came. High above the earth one of the trees was being thrashed about by a strong wind from the north. Suddenly I heard great snapping sounds as the high limbs of the great tree began to break and started falling. Then the giant trunk snapped and the whole tree was crashing toward the earth. I turned quickly to the east and started to run when I saw that the entwined trees were being broken by the first falling tree. The trees were crashing in the east and I could not run in that direction. Instantly I turned to the south and started to run. But again the trees in that direction began to be broken by the others and were falling. By now the sound was horrendous as a great roar of snapping and crashing was everywhere. I turned to the west and it was crumbling as well. As a cloud of thick dust began to rise and fill the air around me, I instinctively ran a few steps and dove to the trunk of one of the great trees. I wrapped myself up against it and nestled up against the huge trunk as the roar of crashing continued and the dust boiled covering the entire scene.

    I was unharmed and crawled out after the dust settled through the mass of tangled broken limbs to view a totally new scene. Not one tree, not even a very high trunk, or a very large piece of a tree was left. The entire magnificent forest was only a huge area of broken smashed pieces fit only for fire wood. It was still a bright sunny day with only a few wispy white clouds in the sky but all the sense of protection and comfort no longer existed.

    As I awoke from this dream I was very moved and somewhat afraid. I knew beyond any doubt that the dream was a prophetic word from God and could instantly think of many negative fearful possible interpretations. But I am not usually used as a prophet of doom and was afraid to ask God the meaning. I really was not ready to know the full meaning of this dream and waited a day before asking God to reveal the interpretation of the dream to me.

I cautiously approached God with questions like, does this involve religion? I heard "yes", but with a sense that there was more. I asked, "does this involve the economy and political governments"? Again the answer, "yes". Knowing I was now ready God spoke on and said, **"It is the pride and loftiness of man"**.

For many days since this dream I have been consumed with it. Many questions have arisen as I went to the word and continued to seek God's guidance in more fully understanding the meaning of this word. What exactly is the pride and loftiness of man that has stood majestically for centuries and is now coming down? Why were trees used to represent the loftiness of man as opposed to great cities or tall buildings etc.? How does this relate to the glorious revival and the establishment of God's kingdom on earth now? When is this great crashing fall, which takes away the sense of security and comfort of many people?

*Isa 2:17-18: The **loftiness of man** shall be bowed down, And the haughtiness of men shall be brought low; The LORD alone will be exalted in that day, But the idols He shall utterly abolish.*

The loftiness of man makes a great covering for evil works of spiritual harlotry and adultery. Under the canopy of the lofty pride of men and their mighty works is a comfortable place for sin and evil works to prevail.

*Hosea 4:13: They offer sacrifices on the mountaintops, And burn incense on the hills, Under **oaks**, poplars, and terebinths, **Because their shade is good**. Therefore your daughters commit harlotry, And your brides commit adultery.*

Now is the time of great transition from the ways of fallen man to the ways of the kingdom of our God. The lofty pride of mankind is being exposed and soon will be brought down to nothing. The greatest crash ever is eminent as the prideful works of man come crashing down that the works of God's kingdom may flow through humble men and be established upon the earth. The lofty works of man in which we have trusted will crumble before our eyes.

Zec 11:1-2: Open your doors, O Lebanon, That fire may devour your cedars. Wail, O cypress, for the cedar has fallen, ***Because the mighty trees are ruined. Wail, O oaks of Bashan, For the thick forest has come down.***

In the figurative language of the Holy Spirit in Scripture, trees often represent the life structure of a man. Different types of trees have different characteristics and represent different qualities in man. The oak represents strength and long lasting stability. The oak grows slowly but makes a very strong hard wood and is therefore a picture of strong stable men.

Amos 2:9: "Yet it was I who destroyed the Amorite before them, Whose height was like the height of the cedars, ***And he was as strong as the oaks;*** *Yet I destroyed his fruit above And his roots beneath.*

It is vitally important for us to know the difference between the works of the pride and loftiness of man and the wonderful works and blessings of God. It is possible to come to some very frightening and unreal conclusions if we do not discern the blessings of God and the prideful works of man. We must consider carefully what is crashing down and what is being established on earth.

*Isa 2:12-21: For the day of the LORD of hosts shall come upon everything **proud and lofty**, Upon everything **lifted up**; And it **shall be brought low**; Upon all the cedars of Lebanon that are high and lifted up, And upon **all the oaks of Bashan**; Upon all the **high mountains**, And upon all the **hills that are lifted up**; Upon every **high tower**, And upon every **fortified wall**; Upon all the **ships** of Tarshish, And upon all the **beautiful sloops**.*

*The loftiness of man shall be bowed down, And the haughtiness of men shall be brought low; **The LORD alone will be exalted in that day**, But the idols He shall utterly abolish.*

*They shall go into the holes of the rocks, And into the caves of the earth, From the **terror** of the LORD And the **glory** of His majesty, When He arises to shake the earth mightily.*

*In that day **a man will cast away his idols of silver And his idols of gold**, Which they made, each for himself to worship, To the moles and bats, To go into the clefts of the rocks, And into the crags of the rugged rocks, **From the terror of the LORD And the glory of His majesty**, When He arises to shake the earth mightily.*

This is not doom and gloom! This is a marvelous outpouring of the glory of God!

Yes, it is an awesome shaking! But only those things that lift themselves against God are coming down. God is being exalted above all else in the minds and hearts of man and in the entire earth. It is the manifest glory of God that is coming forth in the earth. It is the terror and the **glory of God** from which man is fleeing into the caves, and that causes him to cast away his idols.

The LORD alone will be exalted in that day, But the idols He shall utterly abolish. (Isa 2:17b)

Have we not been praying and ministering to exalt the LORD and abolish idols? Man has made idols of the blessings of God. What does man have that he has not received? God is the source of every great idea of technology or science that has come forth. The many wonderful works of man today are entirely impossible without God. God is the source of all life and understanding. Trees were used in the dream because they show that the great works of man are from God. He grows the trees of mighty men and their works.

You could not be using your computer, nor driving your car, nor flying from place to place, nor watching TV, nor using any of the other marvelous scientific and technical works, if God had not given man a brain and enlightenment to do these works. Some of us would not even be alive if it were not for the wonderful works in the medical field. These and every great work of man, every building, bridge, city, all wealth, and every notable and noble work of man is an intended blessing from God. None of them could have been done without the gifts of God to and in man. Man did not get or do these things on His own. It is not by our own hand we have gotten this wealth.

The gifts of God become lofty works of pride when man believes that he has gained them on his own.

*Deu 8:17-19: "then you say in your heart, **'My power and the might of my hand have gained me this wealth.'***

*"And you shall **remember the LORD your God, for it is He who gives you power to get wealth, that He may establish His covenant** which He swore to your fathers, as it is this day.*

"Then it shall be, if you by any means forget the LORD your God, and follow other gods, and serve them and worship them, I testify against you this day that you shall surely perish.

The things which men do and do not recognize as coming from God and do not give God thanks for become "loftiness and pride" of man and will not stand in the glory of God. The great spiritual harlotry of Mystery Babylon is man's pride and loftiness. It is man worshiping himself and "his works" and all "his riches" above God. (Rev Ch.17&18) It is esteeming the glory of man and what he does above the glory of God.

In science, technology, finance, business, war, defense, religion, government, education, and in every area of man's works today there is much pride and loftiness of man. It will not stand. Only that which honors God shall be exalted in the earth everything else will be brought low.

The gifts of God become idols when men trust in them above the God that gave them.

We must trust in God for all of our needs and not in the wealth and things He has given. It is God who will protect us and provide for our victory in life. However, we also must not reject His great gifts and think of them as evil just because others may trust in them instead of trusting in the God who gave them.

Isa 31:1 Woe to those who go down to Egypt for help, And rely on horses, Who trust in chariots because they are many, And in horsemen because they are very strong, But who do not look to the Holy One of Israel, Nor seek the LORD!

Psa 49:6-7: Those who trust in their wealth And boast in the multitude of their riches, None of them can by any means redeem his brother, Nor give to God a ransom for him.

For I will not trust in my bow, Nor shall my sword save me. But You have saved us from our enemies, And have put to shame those who hated us.

It is God who gives power to get wealth. Wealth and all the blessings of God are for the purpose of establishing His covenant. Wealth and all the grand achievements of man are from God and are to be used for His purposes with great thanksgiving and praise to God for all He has done.

It is the pride of man that perverts the gifts of God and uses them to build his own lofty works and honors himself and not God. Sinful practices permeate the lofty structure and the prideful works become corrupt. The great Babylonian structure of mans lofty works apart from God is corrupted and is coming down.

*Rev 18:1-4: After these things I saw another angel coming down from heaven, having great authority, and **the earth was illuminated with his glory.***

*And he cried mightily with a loud voice, saying, "**Babylon the great is fallen, is fallen, and has become a dwelling place of demons, a prison for every foul spirit, and a cage for every unclean and hated bird!***

*"For all the nations have drunk of the wine of the wrath of her fornication, the kings of the earth have committed fornication with her, **and the merchants of the earth have become rich through the abundance of her luxury.**"*

*And I heard another voice from heaven saying, "**Come out of her, my people, lest you share in her sins, and lest you receive of her plagues.***

Revival is an urgent life and death matter for much of our world today.

The mixed ways of the past will no longer suffice. The mixture of godliness and the pride and loftiness of man is dangerous in God's people. We must become real with ourselves and God about what we really trust in. We can no longer trust in governments that do not honor God. We cannot trust in education that does not honor God. We cannot trust in religion and theology that honors man along with God. We cannot trust in financial structures that do not honor God. We cannot trust in the strength of man for it will all be bowed down.

Psa 20:7-8: Some trust in chariots, and some in horses; But we will remember the name of the LORD our God. ***They have bowed down and fallen; But we have risen and stand upright.***

Those who trust only in God will stand to bring forth the ways and will of God (the kingdom of God) into the earth. Powerful revival among believers by the manifest glory of God is bringing change from trusting in the lofty works of man to trusting only in God.

The values of the past are not the values of today.

The reformation of the church is coming about as pure hearted believers will no longer be led by the mixture of the ways of man with the ways of God. Purity and holiness are coming to new levels as true revival brings total abandonment of the pride and loftiness of man in religion and every area of life.

Men have valued the godless systems of the world which are filled with the pride and loftiness of man. Now pure hearted children of God are growing to value the glory of Almighty God above all else and at all cost.

The anointing of God empowers man for ministry and destroys the yoke of bondage, but the glory of God destroys all pride and loftiness of man. God's glory and man's glory cannot coexist.

In the passing church emphasis age there were two opposite views held regarding the works of man and the gifts of God by many doctrinal groups. Basically everything has been separated into two groups, **sacred** and **secular**. The sacred consisting of those things involving the church and religion and the secular consisting of everything else. In the emerging focus on the kingdom age believers are realizing that this is an improper division. The proper division should be **sacred** and **profane**. Secular is not the opposite of Sacred.

We are learning that God is involved in all life and is quite concerned with, and involved in secular matters as well as church matters. God is involved in working in all of His kingdom. Both a godly farmer growing food to meet needs of mankind and a preacher giving out spiritual food are ministers of God meeting the needs of people.

God uses man and works through man to meet needs of mankind. Man has three basic areas of need. Those which relate to the spirit, those which relate to the soul (mind, will, and emotions), and those which relate to the body. God is concerned with the whole man.

One of the opposing views has been that everything considered secular is dirty and should be avoided as much as possible. Although consorting with secular things to get money for living expenses must be tolerated and is acceptable practice. In this view people often did not recognize the hand and work of God in scientific, technological, and medical developments that meet needs of man.

Though it is true that the pride of man has often contaminated and perverted the use of God's provision through man, the intention of God in giving these good things is to meet the needs of man. In the emerging kingdom emphasis age believers are beginning to work to serve God by serving His people instead of working to gain for themselves. Whether their job is in the church or the marketplace, and whether it meets a spiritual need, or a mental need, or a physical need, it is a work of service to God and the person can be empowered by God to do the work.

Those who consider everything secular to be sinful and refuse to participate in the works of God coming through men may pay a great price. For example, to ignore and refuse the works of medicine because they come though man may cost unnecessary suffering and possibly premature death. To demand that God heal our eyes and refuse to wear the eye glasses He has provided may be rejecting the provision of God. To demand that God heal our cancer without taking advantage of medical provisions God has provided is about like demanding the ability to walk on the water instead of using the bridge man has been given the ability to build.

In the kingdom emphasis age people are learning that every good gift comes from above including those we may have considered as coming from man in the past. To not accept the provisions of God coming through man and to demand that God feed us, heal us, and meet all of our needs miraculously is a religious form of pride and loftiness of man.

The other opposing view is at the other end of the spectrum. This view ignores God as the source and trust in the works of man to meet man's needs apart from God. In this view people give credit to men for the works God has wrought. They may believe in doctors as their only healers and give God no credit for meeting their needs. They trust the doctors to cure cancer without God. This is a secular form of pride and loftiness of man.

One must seek God and His plan in every situation and never accept the word of man over the instruction of God.

BASILEIA LETTER
Number 16

In the kingdom age we are learning to use the gifts God has given us to meet the needs of others, and to give God thanks for all He does through us. The miracles of stunning technology today are no more or no less than other miracles God is doing in the world today. God is to be praised for all of His works and they are to be used according to His will and direction. Everything which is not is being made low. It is much better to trust in God than to trust in even the best of men and his works.

Psa 118:8-9: It is better to trust in the LORD Than to put confidence in man. It is better to trust in the LORD Than to put confidence in princes.

Probably most believers today are not aware of how much they trust in and are involved with the pride and loftiness of man. As the manifest glory of God comes forth in revival and believers experience His presence their values are exposed and changed. Experiencing the presence and glory of God causes everything else to become of less importance. Many are amazed as they come into the glorious presence of God in revival and see for the first time how much pride and loftiness they had.

Revival is God's chosen way to bring down the pride and loftiness of man. Now in this time there is opportunity to come into the presence of God and have our lofty pride purged from us. For those who will not, other severe methods will be employed. Both the **terror** and the **glory** of God can destroy the pride and loftiness of man.

It is urgent that we diligently enter the spiritual war now by finding our place in the mighty revival taking place in our world. Our enemies, the pride and loftiness of man can be pushed down. God is on the move in our world. Get in on revival and help destroy the loftiness of man in the glory of God.

The crashing fall of the pride and loftiness of man is eminent. One way or the other by glory or by terror the presence of God will bring down the pride and loftiness of man soon.

Psa 44:5-7: Through You we will push down our enemies; Through Your name we will trample those who rise up against us. For I will not trust in my bow, Nor shall my sword save me. But You have saved us from our enemies, And have put to shame those who hated us.

BASILEIA LETTER
Number 17

Renewal And The Kingdom of God

Barbara and I have been privileged to visit several areas of our country where major revivals and something called renewals are occurring by the outpouring of the Holy Spirit. There is no doubt in our minds that this is the most significant move of God we have seen in our lifetime. One of the most talked about things we have witnessed is a myriad of physical and emotional manifestations. Renewal, as it is happening today, is seen in a setting of people falling under the power and at the presence of God, along with shaking, crying out, laughing, and often lengthy times laid out on the carpet in a somewhat euphoric state. Many have asked either out loud or within themselves; What is the reason for this? --- Why is God doing these things?

I have been strongly affected by the presence and power of God in these meetings, and have seen many others powerfully changed. Often manifestations and miracles occur during the lively praise and worship time or in the ministry time when people are prayed for by a prayer team or prayer ministers.

Barbara's first encounter with renewal type prayer ministry was so different from what she was accustomed to that it was a bit frightening to her at first. Yet, after experiencing the powerful praise and worship ministry the awareness of God's presence was so powerful to her that she was more than willing to seek prayer ministry. When she was prayed for, she was aware of great internal changes taking place within herself including a sense of some things being pulled out and removed from her and then being replaced with more of the love of God than she had ever before known. These types of changes can make major differences in how a person thinks, acts, and reacts. The changes in Barbara's life are obvious and seem to be permanent. She and others testify of continuing to be changed each time they are ministered to by the Spirit of God in renewal services.

All of the things God does are not without purpose. Great numbers of people are being changed to be more like Jesus in renewal and revival services. The reformation of the church is continuing to take place as people of God are being changed by God through the many experiences of powerful manifestations and miracles in renewal.

God is creating a clean heart and renewing a right spirit within His people.

Psa 51:10-13 KJV: **Create in me a clean heart, O God; and renew a right spirit within me.**

Cast me not away from **thy presence;** *and take not thy* **holy spirit** *from me.*

Restore unto me the **joy** *of thy salvation; and uphold me with* **thy free spirit.**

Then will I teach transgressors thy ways; *and sinners shall be converted unto thee.*

God's purpose for renewal and revival is the establishment of the kingdom of God --- first in His people and then into the world. The kingdom of God is God's government from heaven on earth.

Governments of men on earth come from the spirit and mind of men. What is within the spirit of men, what they think and believe will determine how they govern. Belief systems develop from the people's perspective of reality and become the basis for governing life. First the individual's life is governed by their belief system;

next, families, tribes, communities, cities, states, nations, and eventually the world is governed by the collective belief systems of men. Wars are fought and great pressures are brought to bear as different belief systems seek to rule in the world.

God's plan is now, and has always been since He formed man on the earth, for man to rule the earth --- to carry out the Father's plans and purposes on the earth --- for the will of God to be done on earth as it is in heaven. The government of God (kingdom of God) on earth is brought forth through man by the Holy Spirit from heaven.

The enemy (Satan and his spirits of darkness) seek to rule the earth by infiltrating and affecting the spirits and minds of men. The enemy is referred to as the prince of the power of the air. He seeks to be king and knows he must rule in the hearts of men to rule the world. His goal is destruction of all life and the planet.

The enemy has been effective in perverting the hearts of men and establishing his lying beliefs in the minds of men. Therefore, the earth is now being governed to a large extent by the ways and will of the enemy. The Scripture is clear that the goal of the enemy's rule is destruction, **not** peace on earth and good will toward men. *(John 10:10)*

Prosperity comes to the nation who's God is the Lord. He who seeks first the kingdom of God and His righteous way of doing and being will prosper and cause the earth to prosper. (Psa *33:12*) *(Matt 6:33)*

Many of the ways of thinking and governing on earth, which are now employed and respected by many people including Christians are not God's kingdom way, but are ways subversively implanted by the enemy over the past centuries. Though many of these ways are seen as acceptable and normal by many believers, they lead to disorder, discord, disunity, and eventually death and destruction.

Some of the enemy's ways are obvious and most believers seek to avoid them. But many of the ways implanted by the enemy are more subtle and have over time become accepted as normal good behavior by believers and non believers alike. **The kingdom of God will not be brought forth in the world through men with perverted hearts** --- men who are knowingly or unknowingly following another spirit and ways other than God's.

Therefore it is imperative that the hearts of men be changed to bring forth the new order of the kingdom of God on earth. In a very real and practical sense men must be renewed by the Spirit of God and implanted with the ways of the kingdom of God in place of the ways now functioning in the hearts of men.

RENEWAL and REVIVAL are methods God is employing to create new hearts and a right spirit within men. This is a marvelous work of God not of man. Notice that in Psalm 51, David is **asking God** to create a clean heart within him and to renew a right spirit within him. *(CREATE in me a clean heart, O God; and RENEW a right spirit within me.)*

In the passing church emphasis age, many people fought long and hard seeking to overcome their wrong ways and to obtain a clean heart and a right spirit. In the emerging kingdom age the presence and power of God has come to earth in a greater measure. In many places and among many peoples, the outpouring of the Holy Spirit is bringing a great awakening. As the awesome presence of God manifest many are overcome by the power of God and fall before Him. They are changed by God Himself **creating a clean heart** within them as they lay before Him soaking in His presence. Healings of past wounds and deliverances from wrong spirits are easy in the power and presence of God.

Just as David asked in *Psa 51:10-13,* many are receiving a **clean heart and a renewed right spirit in His PRESENCE** by the Holy Spirit; the JOY of His salvation is being restored, and they are upheld by His free Spirit.

*(Create in me a clean heart, O God; and renew a right spirit within me. Cast me not away from **thy presence**; and take not thy **holy spirit** from me. Restore unto me the **joy** of thy salvation; and uphold me with **thy free spirit**.)*

Many in the past have sought to obtain a clean heart and right spirit by the Word of God but have not had the experience of the Word dwelling among and within them by the presence of God manifest through the Holy Spirit. The study of the Word must lead us to the experience of God to receive the renewal of God. The joy of His salvation comes as we experience His presence.

Just to know something from the Word is not the same as experiencing it.

As we experience God first hand, we will become powerful in teaching transgressors the ways of God and sinners will be converted unto God. Evangelism becomes bringing forth the presence and power of God by the Holy Spirit to touch and impact sinners. Once they experience a touch from the presence of God they can and will accept the Word of God and receive the salvation of God. *(**Then will I teach transgressors thy ways;** and sinners shall be converted unto thee.)*

A great hunger is developing among God's people for purity and holiness in the presence of God.

Especially young people are sensing a great hunger for the clean wonderful experience of the glory of God. Across the world people are crying out for more of God, more of His presence, more of His cleansing, more purity, holiness --- more of the reality of the presence of God and His glory in and around their lives.

The contamination of polluted views and life are very odious to the one who has experienced the glory of God, but seem normal to those who over time have grown accustom to them. This may be likened to a person who first enters an area where the air is greatly polluted with chemicals and waste from uncontrolled industrial emissions. Their eyes burn and their nose throat and lungs hurt and they may gag as they attempt to breathe the contaminated air. Yet the people who have lived in this environment for a time go about their daily business and don't even notice the horrible stench and the caustic chemicals in the air. Much of the world's population, including many Christians, have lived for so long with the pollutions of immorality, greed, selfishness, anger, rage, violence, sexual perversion, drug and alcohol abuse, and filth of every kind, that they have adjusted to it and no longer notice how caustic and vile life has become.

Once they are exposed to the purity of the presence God, and compare life cleansed by the presence of God to life as it has been, they become painfully aware of how impure and polluted their lives and those around them have become. When they taste the purity and glory of God in the reality of experiencing His presence they hunger for more and more of His presence and purifying love. They develope a great distaste for the polluted life of the past and a great desire for the purity and holiness of God.

We now live in a world of people hungering for more of God to continually purify and cleanse their hearts from the pollutants of sin and the bondages of religion. God is calling forth a generation to be cleansed and then to be a part of cleansing the world. Great power and anointing is again being poured out as the apostolic work and government of God is coming forth into the world.

The old structures of church government are giving way as hundreds of thousands and even millions are finding new life and a new way in Christ Jesus. Truly, Jesus is beginning to be recognized as Lord of life and not just Saviour of the soul. First the individual's life is cleansed by the presence of God bringing the work of Christ through the Holy Spirit. Then the church is being cleansed and changed from all the control and traditions of man. All of the perversions of religion are melting as the presence and glory of God is manifesting. God's servants are becoming those without any ambition or desires apart from knowing and pleasing God. Simply to be with Him in His awesome presence --- to bask in His glory --- and to make Him know by bringing others to His awesome presence.

There has never been a time exactly like this and will probably never again be a time in which the presence of God is so mercifully pouring out His grace gifts to change the world. Those who hold to the past and cling tightly to the old church governments and practices filled with the perversions of religion and traditions of men with all their controlling mechanisms, will be greatly upset as were the money changers in the temple when Jesus turned their tables and drove them out. The hierarchy of religious rulers will confront the mighty work of Jesus coming forth with no better results than the leaders had when they questioned Jesus as to by what authority He did these things. In short Jesus told them that it is by the authority of the people who believed. *(Mat 21:23-27)*

The enemy has overplayed his hand. He has brought forth so much filth into our world and churches that he is becoming clearly exposed. The glorious presence of the light of God is shining forth into our dark world and creating a great contrast and providing a beautiful option for the multitudes of people who are trapped in darkness of sin and polluted religion.

Mat 4:16: The people who sat in darkness have seen a great light, And upon those who sat in the region and shadow of death Light has dawned..

Now is the time for every Christian to turn from the wicked ways that have slipped up on us and overtaken us as we have gradually adjusted to the pollution of the enemy in our world. *(2 Chr 7:14)* The wonderful love of God that awaits us in His glorious presence is so much greater than all of our past life that it becomes easy and reasonable to cast off our past with all the works of darkness and embrace the purity and holiness of our loving glorious Father in the great outpourings of His Spirit bringing renewal, revival, and reformation.

Much of the church in the passing church emphasis age has looked forward to the bodily return of Christ or the hope of escaping by death into the wonderful presence of our Lord. God is here to become one with us now. We no longer must wait for a future time or event to be in the glorious presence of God Himself. Now, at this time, in our world, the mighty presence of God is present to love us, heal us, deliver us, to save us to the utmost --- to create within us a clean heart and a right spirit. We can now embrace Him and share our deepest love with Him as His own Bride and become His very own Body in the world.

Freedom develops in the presence of God --- freedom from bondages of sin and its evil addictions that steal the joy and victory of our lives --- freedom from religious bondages that enslave us to forms, rituals, and the manipulation of religious men driven by religious spirits --- freedom to walk in the Spirit and flow the love and power of God to cleanse and heal --- freedom to be renewed and to renew our world by the power and presence of the Spirit and the Word of God. *(John 8:31-32) (Gal 5:16)*

In the passing church age many preached against sin and pronounced the judgment to come for sin with generally very poor results in stopping the invasion of the pollution of our world. There remains today those who see the pollution in our pulpits as well as our people and cry out against it, again with poor results.

In the emerging kingdom age the power and presence of God is made manifest in corporate gatherings. The people and preachers may not even need to be told of sin in their lives or to hear preaching against sin. Their sin is made clear to them in the awesome purity and presence of the glory of God. The great alternative of life in God becomes real to them and sin is clearly seen as sin and easily renounced in favor of the wonderful life of peace and love in the presence of God.

The reason some can only preach negatively against religious manipulation and sin is that they themselves are not yet experiencing the powerful presence of God changing their own lives and flowing through them to change others. Therefore, they have no real positive alternative to offer -- no real standard to hold up by the Spirit of the LORD, that will draw men away from religion and sin and toward purity and holiness in God.

*Isa 59:19: When the enemy comes in like a flood, The **Spirit** of the LORD will lift up a standard against him.*

BASILEIA LETTER
Number 18

Increasing Release of Glory In The Kingdom of God

Joel 2:28-29: *"And it shall come to pass afterward That **I will pour out My Spirit** on all flesh; Your sons and your daughters shall prophesy, Your old men shall dream dreams, Your young men shall see visions.*

And also on My menservants and on My maidservants I will pour out My Spirit in those days."

Isa 9:7: *Of the <u>increase</u> of His government and peace There will be no end, Upon the throne of David and over His kingdom, To order it and establish it with judgment and justice From that time forward, even forever. The zeal of the LORD of hosts will perform this.*

Recently there has been a notable increase in the presence and power of God. There is a continuing increase in intensity and acceleration of the outpouring of the Spirit of God. Burdens that were difficult in the past are more easily moved with the anointing of the Anointed One coming forth through pure hearted believers in this season, as the outpouring of God is establishing His kingdom on earth as it is in heaven.

Across the world many believers are uniting and coming together to pray for revival in our world. These prayer and worship gatherings are often visited mightily by the presence of God demonstrating the power of the gospel of the kingdom with miracles and changed lives. Life is being poured out and people, old and young, are prophesying the message of God with power and accuracy. Faith seems greater and more easily obtainable than ever before. Now, in this emerging kingdom emphasis age, it seems easy to believe the things that Christians once struggled to believe in the passing church emphasis age. We have entered a new season on earth.

Things are changing rapidly as this era becomes more evident with each step of increasing intensity and acceleration. One of those steps was made very apparent to a small group, of which I was a part, gathered in the city of Greensboro, NC USA, for the purpose of seeking the face of God and praying for an outpouring of God's Spirit to bring revival in the mid-Atlantic region of the USA. As prayer was being made it was as if someone turned up the power of God switch to several times as much as it was before.

These prayer meetings were the first held by the group. They were ordered by the Lord as individually people were instructed to come together in Greensboro on this date to pray for revival. Not being of Jewish heritage, no one was aware at the time of receiving their instruction to come and pray, that it was Rosh Hashanah, the Jewish new year. The prayer began on Friday night September 10, 1999 and was continued the next morning of September 11, 1999.

In the Friday night session the presence of God became intense during a season of corporate prayer. The power of God moved in to heal and without laying on of hands or individual prayer, healings began to occur. The next morning a 79 year old man testified that when healing the heart was mentioned in the prayer he suddenly had the faith to reach out and receive healing of a bad heart valve. He had not been able to walk more than a few steps without stopping to breathe. The next morning he walked about the equivalent of two city blocks without even breathing hard.

This was just the warm up as the power of God was turned up in the Saturday morning prayer session. We were aware of the change as God spoke in our hearts that we had entered a new season, not just in this little group but world wide there was a shift, an increase that had to do with the Jewish new year and the new millennium.

Since that day, God has confirmed with the words of prophets in different places the intensification and acceleration taking place at this time and moving us toward the most awesome time on earth. Since that time, not only is much prophecy coming forth but also much revelation is coming forth to the apostles who have an ear to hear. Even the Book of Revelation which has been so difficult and so often interpreted erroneously in parts rather than as a whole, is being revealed as the covers are further being removed in these days. The mighty army of God spoken of in Joel 2 is clearly seen to be coming forth in this day as the Book of Revelation, which was written to be understood in this time is opening before us.

If you are reading this, you are alive in a day of major history of God being written in the earth. There has never before been a time like this time. It is indeed similar to the time of the first century but it is becoming even a greater time as the fruit of the seeds planted in the first century are now coming forth. The works that Jesus did, shall you who believe now do. The sum total of the works bought forth by Christ in believers will exceed those done in His earthly body and are the glory of God --- no longer just the hope of glory. *"Christ in you the hope of glory"* is becoming Christ in you the glory of God now.

A TIME OF WAR
By: Chuck D. Pierce (excerpt only)

This is such an exciting time for the Body of Christ. I believe with the beginning of Rosh Hashanah we shifted into a new, historical time frame in the Body of Christ. At this millennial shift, change and conflict are abounding throughout the earth at such an accelerated pace that we find ourselves groping for stability, footing, and positioning. The world is changing so quickly that many awaken with anxiety to each new day. Societal institutions are shifting at such a pace that from region to region the entire earth seems to be in a constant state of "earthquake". A word synonymous with conflict is "warfare". That war is the clash with an enemy, whether of a tangible nature or a discerned perception. God, the Omnipotent Creator of the universe and mankind, always has had a remnant leadership that arises in the midst of conflict, activating their faith and determining the course of events that molds the world for generations to come. God has a priesthood, a nation above all nations, that He draws near to Him and communicates His kingdom desires, so His Victory goes forth on the earth. He then says to this priesthood of believers, called the Church: "Rise Up and War until you see My purposes for this generation established!"

SPIRITUAL EARTHQUAKE IN BUENOS AIRES
By: Pastor J. Conrad Lampan

September 11th (Rosh Hashanah) something very unusual happened in Buenos Aires, Argentina: Over 450,000 evangelicals of ALL denominations gathered at a main street (The widest street of the world -- 120 meters wide). The crowd covered several blocks. **At 3:59 PM when they were praying the area was SHAKEN!**

All the evangelical churches were participating in unity such that pastors did not want to give their names, no list of personalities was read: it was only the Body of Christ praying in unity. At 3:59 the place was shaken.In many houses/apartments furniture was moved from its place. Interestingly enough the places that seemed to be more affected by the quake were those of the press: radios,

TV stations, and newspapers. They called the seismic office to inquire about a possible movement in San Andres fault and their system had not registered any earth movement. Some of them suggested that the sound from the audio system and the crowd shouting might have produced the quake but then one remembered that many political meetings have taken place there with much louder noise and nothing happened. Some newspaper reported: "curiously at that exact time the evangelicals were praying". The media can try many explanations but we know what happened: *"And when they had prayed the place where they were assembled together was shaken" Act 4:31*

Editors Note: The following prophetic word is very comprehensive regarding all facets of the current increase in the outpouring of God since Rosh Hashanah September 11, 1999.

WORD OF SEPTEMBER 26th, 1999
By Mark Wattenford

GOD' GLORY POSITIONED OVER GOD'S PEOPLE

Behold the promises of God are true and faithful. What He has spoken He shall perform. **The glory and the power has positioned itself over Gods people and the fullness of it is complete and lacking nothing,** though the hearts of Gods people wonder if it shall be sufficient to meet their expectations and the word of the Lord is, "Prepare thyself, for it shall not only meet your expectations but those things I shall bring shall over take your hearts and the abundance of the blessings that SHALL BE poured out shall be overflowing". I come with my reward with me, to call forth my chosen vessels, to bestow on them the authority that I send them forth with. Behold the authority and the power I shall open up upon my chosen vessels, how great it is and full of glory. They shall indeed be the sons of glory who shall walk in this hour - in my spirit. And look at those who shall be stirred to jealousy because of those whom I have chosen. For those who are full of themselves have I not chosen and they shall wax cold in their hearts because of those whom I HAVE chosen.

ANOINTING WITHOUT MEASURE

In this hour my vessels shall walk as I walked in the earth, with an anointing that is without measure... not a portion, nor a double portion, but a portion that is without measure. Those things that were done in the past will be commonly done and many things that have never been done before will be done so that the world may come to have no excuse before God in that they shall see the works of God in full view and they shall be without excuse when they will openly reject God and they will therefore seal themselves for the judgment that shall soon after come.

COMMUNION OPENS MYSTERIES

Rise up in song my people for I shall walk among you as never before and the communion I shall have with my people shall be an open communion. The light of my glory shall rest upon the sons of God. **I shall sit among my people and speak to them the mysteries of the kingdom and I shall walk among them as they rise up and go forth. The books of the prophets NOW shall all be opened up, and the mysteries of them shall be fully brought forth into light.** The Pharisees have said that all mysteries have been revealed and that there are no new things to know... I shall bring forth such revelation of my word as never before seen and I shall shake every Pharisee with a quaking so that many shall fear what is coming forth in my word and in my revelation of my word.

THE NEW GENERATION ARMY

Behold I bring forth a shaking in the heavens and a shaking upon the earth. **I shall gather my people unto me and I shall take captive this new generation and shall draw them unto me and shall make of them the second wave of my armies.** Though they are young they shall wield the sword of my word and shall strike with accuracy that which the sword was meant to strike. I am raising up voices of thunder all over the world; voices that shall speak mightily like the world has never known. The fear of these thunders shall be wide spread and the dread of their coming forth shall pierce the hearts of men.

PROMOTION OF THE FAITHFUL

Behold, my reward is with me, to bestow upon the faithful what is due them. To promote my vessels that have remained in me - to greater places in me. The mantle of authority shall rise up in the earth as it has never been before. The sons of God and the Sons of Thunder are brought forth. They shall tear down strongholds with violence. They shall have no mercy upon the spirits that bind. They shall not give ear to demons or suffer the doctrines of men to take my people captive any longer. The day of deliverance is come to my people and I shall bring them fully out from captivity of the doctrines of men, the doctrines of demons and the traditions wherein they have been bound.

INCREASING GLORY

The cloud of my glory has formed and is positioned above my people and it is even now sending forth a light rain, but I say... this light rain is NOT for long as this cloud of my spirit and glory shall be rent and the pouring out of it shall catch all in surprise and it will be as a flood upon you where you stand.

The day shall rise with the light of its shining and all things hidden shall be revealed. The spirits that had power in darkness shall no longer have power as they shall be uncovered and brought into the light and judgment of my glory and my light. The dead shall rise, the blind shall see, the deaf shall hear, the lame shall walk, the sick shall rise up and they shall know again the Good shepherd that I am.

JUDGMENT OF SHEPHERDS

I shall not beat them as the hirelings have that have been over my people. And I come to judge them that have been over my sheep that have raised their hand up against my lambs and have beaten them and without mercy. Shall I not beat them who have beaten my sheep? Shall I give mercy unto those who have not shown mercy upon my lambs? I shall tear down with violence these kingdoms that these wicked shepherds have built for themselves. Repent you fallen shepherds who have built for yourselves kingdoms from the very blood I shed. Repent and turn lest I take the very stones of your own kingdom and cast them upon you, to destroy you and remove you from the earth. And why do you say I shall not remove you from the earth? I tell you I shall remove many from the earth in this hour who have offended me and have taken my name in vain and have beaten my sheep. I tell you the truth, it is YOU who have taken my name in vain, who have built up kingdoms for yourself and have bartered with the evil one that you might fill your bellies with the desires of your flesh and have paid for your lusts with the very cross of my death. My death was for the souls of men, but you have eaten it up to consume it and to use it for the desires of your lusts and the things of the flesh.

APOSTLES ESTABLISHED

The day of my rising is come. My prophets hear my voice.

I have now established the apostles of my choosing in the earth. They shall rise up and go forth and bring structure to my kingdom on earth. They have deep hearts of mercy, but they shall go forth and destroy what hinders my kingdom from coming forth. I tell you to search your hearts and ask of me whether it be filled with light or darkness, for there are too many who think they do not stand in my way, but who do stand in my way and are set for a breaking. Some I shall remove from their place and shall take them home because they have not heard my voice in this time and who stand in the way of my spirit. I am a God of Love and it is a long suffering love, but I will not suffer ruin to my kingdom in this time and I shall remove them that stand in the way. Those vessels I bring forth shall rise up with wings as eagles, they shall run and not grow weary, they shall walk and not grow faint. Some vessels I will raise up that men will not be able to kill. Were men to kill them, they shall rise up from death to continue. Time and time again they shall rise up. They shall not be taken off the earth unless I say. For all the sacrifices my people have offered up over many years, I bring now the reward for their giving. In this time those who have given up lands I shall increase and give them portions of the earth. Men shall deliver up riches into the storehouses of my people. I shall rebuke the devourer in this time and for a season he shall have no power to come against my chosen ones. I shall shut the mouth of the devourers as I shut the mouth of the Lions before Daniel.

CHILDREN MINISTER IN POWER

Your young children shall speak prophecy and have visions and I have appointed even them to witness and to preach the word of the kingdom in this time. They shall see my angels coming forth and with angels they shall speak and converse on many things. Think not slight of them or think them of little value for they are precious in my sight and I shall put words of wisdom in these young vessels. They shall win souls into the kingdom through the purity of their hearts and the anointing I shall cover them with in wisdom. Speak to the darkness that has bound your families and I shall chase off the darkness that before has had place and rule in your houses. I shall rise up as a mighty and angry lion and shall run after darkness and shall chase it and drive it from my people.

HEAVENS OPENED

The earth has never seen before the heavens as it shall be opened up before my people. As Stephen saw the heavens opened so shall the people of God behold the heavens opened and the glory of my coming. The earth is mine and I now am risen up to take into possession all that is mine. The heavens are mine and I shall possess all that is in the heavens. I shall place my foot on the head of the serpent and for a season he shall not come against my chosen ones. I shall break the teeth of the lions who seek to come against mine anointed and the fear of my judgments shall come upon the hearts of men.

REMOVE ROBES OF RELIGION

To those who have the heart of Nichodemus who do hunger after me, I say... **remove the robes of your positions and the flatteries of men and follow after me and I shall give you instead the robe of righteousness and of holiness that you may enter into these things I bring into the earth.**

JUDGE WITH MERCY

To those who judge... seek my counsel while it is yet early that you may judge according to my counsel, lest I find that you are without mercy and I come to judge you. For those I find in this hour who have no mercy I shall strike with an iron rod in my anger. In this time the earth shall know the anger of God and the wrath of His displeasure for in the open I shall openly stand before them and offer mercy this last time and those who refuse I shall openly destroy before the eyes of many. The hearts of men shall fail them in this hour for the fear that shall come over them. Listen to my cry all yee nations, listen and know that I AM the lamb of God that was slain for your sake and none shall stand before my father who shall reject me. You shall NOT know God who refuse to know me and seek after my face.

HONOR FOR TRUE SERVANTS

My prophets I shall honor in this time and I shall make many jealous who think in themselves they have honored me and they have not. I shall pour upon my prophets blessings that shall anger those who think in themselves that they possess the kingdom of heaven and they do not. This is the day of the song of the prophets, but who can know what that means? This is the day of the power of the coming forth of my apostles. My arm shall strike the earth in judgment and the whole of it shall shake. Woe to them who say they possess my kingdom and do not, who say all things continue as with their fathers and everyday shall be as the other and God shall not move as these prophets say. You have not given heed to my chosen ones. You think in yourselves you are my counsel and I say, brace yourselves if you can for I shall shake all that can be shaken and if you hold on to anything that is not me you shall be carried off with the shaking.

DELIVER QUICKLY THOSE WHO ARE BOUND

Why do you not hear my voice, why do you not seek my face, why do you withstand the voice of my prophets, why do you not show mercy to them that are bound and even add further chains to them that are bound? For in this my anger is kindled greatly, that you have NOT brought liberty to the captive as I ordered you to do, but rather you have bound up further them that were in bonds. My wrath is kindled greatly because of this and I say... **run to them, run to them that you have bound and lose them quickly before I come and find that you have not done so.** I tell you the wrath of my anger for this is ALL consuming and I shall not have mercy on them who have done this when I am come and find they have not done as I said, and loosed them who are in captivity. You have but a short time to repent and right these things and you must RUN to lose them that you have bound for I come quickly and shall without mercy judge you if you have not done as I have said. Loose them who are bound!!

GOVERNMENT OF GOD

The kingdom shall be on earth as it is in Heaven. I bring the government of my Father among men. That which is in Heaven shall be seen on earth. My glory is come that it may enter into my people and that it may rest upon my chosen vessels. I shall raise up my temple of living stones. I go forth throughout the earth establishing my vessels and putting in place the stones of my temple. Who shall hear the words of my prophets and who are they who shall not be offended by the words of my apostles in this hour? There is a harvest and an ingathering that has never been before until now. A multitude shall rise up and enter into the kingdom as a field going forth from horizon to horizon. I shall remove striving from my people and I shall be in them with the power they have sought and yearned for. Before one shall finish praying I will have done it for them. Rise up and rejoice, for all things are come to be fulfilled and from this time forward you, my people, shall enter into all that is in me and you shall go forward in me unto the day that my kingdom is fully brought forth upon the earth.

BASILEIA LETTER
Number 19
Time of The Kingdom of God

Is it now time for the manifestation of the kingdom of God from heaven on earth -- time for the will of God to be done on earth as it is in heaven?

As we all know God is supreme over all creation including all the earth and all that is on the earth. So then why and how is it that the will of God -- the kingdom of God is not fully observed upon the earth? How is it that man can walk outside the will of Almighty God in disobedience to God and His ways? How can it be that the enemy kingdom or principality can exsert its self and its ways on earth? Is God with His omnipotent power and supreme wisdom unable to overrule the enemy and his ways? Is it not true that all of creation is under the rule of God who created it and His Son Jesus through whom all things were created and now consist?

*Col 1:16b-17a: **All things were created through Him (Jesus) and for Him. And He is before all things, and in Him all things consist.***

Rev 4:11: "*You are worthy, O Lord, To receive glory and honor and power;* ***For You created all things, And by Your will they exist and were created.***"

John 1:3: ***All things were made through Him, and without Him nothing was made that was made.***

All creation heavenly and earthly was created and continues to exist and consist in order by the exerted energy of God. Everything created exist by the power and design of God through Christ Jesus. Christ Jesus has complete authority and therefore control over all creation--- He is before all things.

*Col 1:15-19: **He (Christ Jesus) is the image of the invisible God, the firstborn over all creation. For by Him all things were created that are in heaven and that are on earth, visible and invisible, whether thrones or dominions or principalities or powers. All things were created through Him and for Him. And He is before all things, and in Him all things consist.***

*And He is the head of the body, the church, who is the beginning, the firstborn from the dead, that **in all things He may have the preeminence. For it pleased the Father that in Him all the fullness should dwell.***

There is nothing impossible to Christ Jesus. The creator is fully able to recreate or change any part of creation, including things like bringing the truth of God's love and salvation to anyone --- healing deformed or diseased bodies--- or redistributing the wealth of the world in accordance with His will and purpose.

Man's part is to bring God's desires into the world by connecting with God and **hearing and obeying** the will of God. As God shows man things in the world which He desires to change, man has the ability to PRAY and take the desired change to God; and then to become an instrument in His hand to change the situation in connection with the power of God from heaven.

My friend and prayer partner, Billy, is used in intercession and is prone to be led away for hours or days of prayer and/or into divine encounters for ministry. One afternoon I was waiting for Billy to arrive at my log cabin in the East Texas rural area. He had called and said he would be there at a certain time. He arrived hours later than expected and told the following story.

God had directed him to take a sort of back trail way to get to my cabin instead of the usual way. He thought that it was just for a pleasant scenic diversion. But as he approached a travel trailer where a woman was sitting out front, God spoke to him to pull in and tell her about Jesus. It surprised Billy and wanting to be sure, he did not stop but drove by and stopped at the first opportunity to consider the situation. Being a man and alone in a rural area he was concerned that in might frighten the woman. Again it was made clear to him to go tell the woman about Jesus.

As soon as Billy started talking to the woman it was obvious that she was very distraught as she began sharing her situation with him. She had recently gotten out of prison for shooting and killing her abusive husband and was having a very hard time adjusting to life again. Nothing was working out for her and she did not know what to do.

Billy was able to tell her that God had sent him to help her. She was gloriously saved and her countenance instantly changed. Billy told her she needed to tell someone about her salvation. She thanked him and instantly took off to go tell her sister who was a believer.

In the weeks that followed the woman was very excited about her new found life and spent much time in the Word and prayer and had great fellowship with her sister and in church. It was later learned that her cousin had been crying out to God for the woman's salvation and asking God to send someone.

After several weeks of excited new life the woman suddenly dropped dead from a heart attack. She was only in her thirties and she nor anyone else knew of the illness. Billy shared how God had provided for her salvation and was a great witness to her family.

Because the cousin was connected to God within she could see the need of the woman and cry out to God to send someone. Because Billy was connected to God within and because he was willing to obey he was led at the precise time and to the precise place to deliver the love of Jesus and make an eternal difference.

These kinds of stories of men and women sent of God to make a difference in the lives of people and the world could be told many times over. Simple ordinary people who are connected and empowered by the Spirit of God.

Powerful ministries, churches, kingdom businesses, and nations can all be formed and reformed by the power of God. Nothing is impossible to the Christ within us as long as time remains.

Psa 104:30 You send forth Your Spirit, they are created; And You renew the face of the earth.

There was a man a number of years ago whom God directed to give money to send people with the good news to the lost world. This man worked for hourly wages and had a family of several children to support. He could give very little. He cried out to God to help him earn money to reach the lost. A series of miraculous events occurred as he continued to seek God. Job situations began to change and soon the man with only a high school education was earning as much in a day as he had earned in a week.

As he remained faithful to give and to continue to seek God, doors continued to open and soon he was the owner of a small business. As the man continued to pray, God would speak His desires for the little business and give instruction as to what to do next. In three years the little company had become a multi million dollar corporation, was free of debt, and was used in supplying funds for ministries to reach the lost.

In a recent report from a small village in India a visiting ministry team wrote the following in their report. "We saw many instantaneous, miraculous healings. One in particular struck me. A mother and father brought a little girl to me, probably about four years old. **They pulled up her shirt and showed that her stomach was distended in a terrible way. As I laid hands on her and prayed we saw her stomach go completely flat!** The God of mercy had shown Himself graceful to this little one. How great He is!"

The next day they wrote the following in their report. "The people drank in the teaching about the heart of the Father and were enthralled with the reality of a God who is interested in relationship, not religion. When the time for commitment came 35 Hindus, 25 women and 10 men, stood to their feet without hesitation to renounce all gods except Jesus. Two of these men were very advanced in years and had been strong in the Hindu religion. So in light of the fact that there were only 25 believers in the village before, there was some phenomenal church growth! Then we had the people line up for prayer and once again saw instantaneous, miraculous healings. **A child was brought to me with boils on his legs. Before my very eyes Jesus shrank them away to nothing.**"

There is nothing in all of creation that is above the Lord Jesus. He is the undisputed Lord of all and is the full expression of the Father. Jesus and the Father have the omnipotent ability to make any decision without any limitation. There is no force, no power strong enough to defy or challenge the decisions of God. Nothing can contradict or refute a decision made and spoken by God.

Phil 2:9-11: ***Therefore God also has highly exalted Him and given Him the name which is above every name****, that at the name of Jesus every knee should bow, of those in heaven, and of those on earth, and of those under the earth, and that every tongue should confess that **Jesus Christ is Lord, to the glory of God the Father.***

Among the important decisions made by God regarding earth and mankind, two massively important decisions of immense magnitude have been made by Jesus and the Father. These two decisions have, and will continue to affect all existence on Planet Earth for all time.

The first awesome decision was made by Father God. **Father God decided to share the rule of earth with man. He gave man dominion on earth and limited Himself to the will of man regarding the life and fate of mankind and all creation on earth. God gave man a free will and the ability to choose. God, by His own decision limited Himself on earth by what man would decide.**

The second awesome decision was made by the man Christ Jesus. **Jesus decided to do only according to the Father's will and not according to His human will as a man. He decided to be obedient to the Father's will and do only what He heard and saw the Father doing.** *(John 5:19)*

Phil 2:5-8: Let this mind be in you which was also in Christ Jesus, who, being in the form of God, did not consider it robbery to be equal with God, but made Himself of no reputation, taking the form of a bondservant, and coming in the likeness of men. ***And being found in appearance as a man, He humbled Himself and became obedient to the point of death, even the death of the cross.***

This is the decision that man should have made with his free will. But man instead decided to disobey the will of the Father in favor of his own will. Every decision of man that is not according to the will of God leads toward death (destruction, disorder, separation from the presence of God). Every decision made in accordance with the will of God leads toward life (prosperity, order, and the presence of God). Only in **time** of the existence of creation has God given dominion of earth to man. Man can decide which kingdom will rule earth -- the kingdom of God and light or the false kingdom of darkness of the evil one.

The potential for the kingdom of God ruling earth through man was redeemed by the man Christ Jesus, establishing again the will of God being performed by man on earth. Jesus became obedient even to the cross and provided that which was and is necessary for the redemption of mankind and the reestablishment of the kingdom of God on earth. Christ Jesus now lives in redeemed pure hearted believers to again bring man and all things over which man has dominion into alignment with the will of Father.

Time is a measurement of the continuation of created existence.

Along with height, width, depth, density, frequency or speed, time is a dimension of created life and existence. All creation emanates from God. Every created thing investigated to its deepest origin and simplest form will break down at some point and disappear into the spiritual realm as only energy from God.

If one investigates any item which consist of any materials, which are made of elements, which can be broken down into molecules, and then into atoms, and then into atomic structure of neutrons, protons, and electrons, which at some point in the investigation cease to be matter and are seen as energy, which can only emanate from God Himself the creator of all that exist.

Time and seasons are built into the natural creation of God. Physical and chemical activities act and react with one another in certain patterns and establish the existence of measurable time. Natural growth, degeneration, regeneration, movement and mass are all functions of change tied to time. Time and change are forever linked together. As long as creation remains, time remains. As long as time remains, change remains. There cannot be creation without time and there cannot be time without change.

There can be no matter without energy and there can be no energy without God. All energy and therefore all creation exist by the will of, and under the full authority of God. God and only God can alter the patterns of time and every other dimension or measure of created existence. God who is Spirit has complete and full authority and ability to alter all dimensions or measures of creation without limit. Therefore Spirit (God) rules over all creation (physical).

However, on the planet on which we live God has chosen to link His Spirit with man and to work or operate with the will of man. Spirit rules physical. Physical does not rule spiritual. The only way physical can effect the spiritual is through the Spirit in man.

Man is the only created being on earth which has a natural earthly body and a living Spirit within. The mind relates to the earth -- the earthly or physical realm and the Spirit relates to God in the spiritual realm. The connection or interface of the two in the heart of man is the Spirit /physical or God/man working together to rule on this planet.

Everything on this planet exist, consist in order, and is changed by the will and exerted energy (power) of God. Only man is given the opportunity to hear God from the spiritual realm and speak to God from the physical realm to the spiritual realm. Only man has the God given place of connecting with God and interfacing between Spirit God and physical creation. Only man working with God has the power to change the earth and things on earth to conform to the will of God from the spiritual realm. **God can do anything through man; and man can do anything through God, if both are willing.**

The kingdom of God is within redeemed man. As Christ Jesus abides in man and man abides in Christ Jesus the authority and power of God flows upon the earth to bring the will of God from heaven to earth. Christ in man will do as He did when He was on earth in his natural body. He will remain connected to the Father and do only what He hears and sees the Father doing.

All of creation must respond to the word of Christ Jesus flowing through redeemed purified man on earth now in this time. This is the **Time of The Kingdom of God.** Christ Jesus is now in this day being manifest in men, women, and children to change our world and bring forth the kingdom of God from heaven, to cause the will of God to be done on earth as it is in heaven.

The mighty river of the outpouring of the Spirit of God in our day is for the purpose of redeeming and purifying rebellious man so that the glory of God will be manifest into our world and the kingdom of God from heaven will rule the earth. The kingdoms of this world are becoming the kingdoms of our God as men are changed by the powerful presence of God and are empowered to hear and obey the Father.

Faith is being birthed in the earth as the hearts of man are bursting forth with the overflowing life of God in Christ Jesus flowing by the Holy Spirit out into the world as rivers of living water flooding the earth with the love and plan of God.

This is the **Time of The Kingdom of God** coming forth on earth. The time in which nothing is impossible as multitudes are swept up in the river of the love of God filling and changing millions of people. The youth of our world today will see the mighty hand of God flow in their lives and in our world in a way people of the past have dreamed and prophesied about but were not able to experience in their day. All the saints of the past will be fulfilled as the mighty return to the ways of our King, the kingdom of God lifestyle rules in the earth.

The powerful presence of God and the rivers of living water are coming forth from Christ in man to show forth the glory of God and establish His kingdom.

"Christ in you the hope of Glory"

BASILEIA LETTER
Number 20

Family And The Kingdom of God

Jesus is the head of the great family of God. The patterns of the universal family of God are the kingdom of God patterns for governing all institutions of life on earth including families, tribes, churches, businesses, states, and nations.

*Eph. 3:14-17: For this reason I bow my knees to the Father of our **Lord Jesus Christ, from whom the whole family in heaven and earth is named**, that He would grant you, according to the riches of His glory, to be strengthened with might through **His Spirit in the inner man, that Christ may dwell in your hearts through faith**; that you, being **rooted and grounded in love**,---*

For centuries men have sought to successfully govern life with systems devised from the intellect of man. For the most part, in recent history, man has elected to ignore the kingdom of God patterns for governing. In the USA, an effort by some has been largely successful in eliminating God and His kingdom patterns from government and establishing substitute humanistic patterns. These perverted patterns devised by intellect and influenced by demons have spread to many nations around the world. In this kingdom emphasis age man must come to the patterns of God for governing life and begin to establish God's kingdom ways on earth.

God's basic pattern for all government is His kingdom family pattern. The family is the core of the kingdom of God governments on earth. The patterns established by God for family are the only ones that will really work in governments, businesses, churches, homes, and other governing institutions. All of life on earth must eventually come into the plan and patterns of God as His kingdom comes and His will is done on earth as it is in heaven.

Like many others, I grew up planted with the worldly patterns of family presented to me in the home of my parents. I did not realize that my family lifestyle was far from the kingdom of God way. Later in life it was shocking to me to find out that the stress and fear of my childhood was not the only way. A child tends to think that the ways of his or her home is normal and the same for all others --- that the lack of unconditional love and the disorder with its conflicts and power struggles is the normal pattern for family. As the child grows and experiences other situations he may become aware that all families are not the same.

I grew up quickly and was anxious to get out of the nagging, fighting, unhappy environment. At the age of seventeen I married and left five of my six younger siblings trapped in the family setting. My sister just younger than myself had already married at fifteen to seek a better life.

I did not know God nor did I have any idea that He had a kingdom plan for life and family. I only knew that surely something would be better than what I had. I vowed that my home would not be like the one I grew up in. Certain things that stressed me as a child would never be allowed in my family.

Though I had a desire for a better way, the patterns of life planted in me and the lack of God's ways in my life caused me to reproduce many of the same patterns. Coming to know God and His saving grace at twenty one years of age began to change everything. But it would be many years and much heart ache before God's kingdom family pattern would become known to me and begin to be established in my life.

The same type scenario was played out in my work life. Again, like others, I assumed that the principles trained into me by family, school, and job experience were the way to do things. Only later as

God began to reveal His kingdom family pattern for business, was I able to achieve much greater levels of prosperity and happiness than ever imagined.

The kingdom of God patterns for living on earth seem idealistic to most people today. Even for many Christians they seam too idealistic and difficult to implement into practical life. For the most part the people of the world have become so ingrained with substitute ways that the ways of God seem strange and sometimes frightening to them. However, the patterns and ways of the world which have been inspired by the enemy may seem natural and practical to them. In the kingdom emphasis age we will experience a change from the perverted ways of man to the establishment of the kingdom family pattern as the foundation for governing all institutions.

Righteousness, peace, and joy are characteristics of the government of God The people of the world seek peace and joy. Yet, for the most part they have ignored the source of peace and joy -- the kingdom of God lifestyle.

Now is the time of restoration to the righteousness, peace, and joy that only comes from the kingdom of God. The great facades and empty shells of seeking to govern life from the intellects of men are coming down. The kingdom of God reality and fullness of life are coming forth as the world endures the greatest change in modern history. It is the transition from the empty rule of man without God to the fullness of the kingdom of God ways ruling in and through man. It is the return to the patterns of God being reinstituted into the world. The people of earth by the thousands upon thousands must be reprogrammed with the patterns of God instead of the patterns of the enemy. The patterns of the enemy have been implanted through profane living and godless education into the foundations of all the world and have fostered many false beliefs and religions.

Only the power and glory of God can eliminate the influence of false beliefs and religions. The acceptance of the practice of false religions will be dissolved by the mighty miracle working life changing presence and glory of almighty God. As the power of God openly defeats diseases, destroys depression, and replaces the work of the enemy with righteousness, peace, and joy, the false beliefs and religions will be exposed as empty, powerless, shells.

Governments will no longer give equal status to false beliefs and religions when the glory and power of God is made manifest and undeniably demonstrated in the world. The governments of the world will no longer outlaw God and His kingdom ways from schools, and government institutions. Government officials will no longer use the excuse that all religions are equal and one must allow them all if one allows the true God to rule in the affairs of men and state. The mighty outpouring of God and the glorious undeniable manifestations of God Himself working through pure hearted men and women will change the world by changing individual lives. There may be very little success in trying to change the governments of the world until the people of God are changed and flowing in the river of the life changing glory and power of Almighty God.

The mighty outpouring of God's Spirit bringing renewal and eventually great revival to the world is preparing the hearts of man to receive and to begin to live the kingdom of God lifestyle. The kingdom family pattern must be learned and implemented into our lives and the lives of our children. The enemy's false patterns will be destroyed by the implementation of God's kingdom family pattern. The enemy's plan to destroy the kingdom of God governments of the world by perverting the family with his false patterns will be foiled.

The great spiritual family of God begins with the Father -- the giver of all life -- the creator of all existence -- the all powerful all loving God. The Son is the mediator between Father God and man -- the redeemer saviour -- head and Lord of all -- the husband of the Bride. The Bride is the purified church -- the New Jerusalem -- the ruling city of the Israel of God -- the mother of the children of God. The children are those born of the union of Jesus and His Bride and are in the process of growing up to maturity.

The patterns of the great family of God are the same for the natural family on earth. God has only one plan for governing-- only one kingdom family pattern. Everything else is either a perversion of God's plan or a counterfeit from the enemy.

God made man in His own image and gave man dominion over the earth. He made man and all the living things on earth from the soil of the earth, except for one thing. Woman was not made from the soil but was made from man. Man only, was created and he was created male and female. There is male man and female man. They are all of one creation. They each are given different equipment for different jobs and functions in the family of God. But each are the same to God spiritually.

The patterns for family are evident in *Genesis, Chapter 2 Amp.* God's pattern is that **before man has his mate** he is to: (1) have spiritual life breathed into him, (2) be walking in close communion with God daily, (3) have a good occupation and instruction for doing it, and (4) depend on revelation from God for direction for his life. **God's pattern is for man to be properly related to Him and established in His purpose before marriage.**

The wife is to be formed from the husband. Only woman was made "built up" from another living creature (man). The husband is the source of life to the wife. He must receive life from God and bring it to the wife. The instruction for the family's direction and spiritual life comes through the husband.

Therefore, a man must **leave** his father and mother and **cleave** to his wife, and become one flesh with her. She is to become his *"helper - meet, suitable, adapted, completing for him"*. He has the vision, the instruction, and the occupation or business direction from God. **She is to adapt to him, not him to her.** She is to become suited to him.

Many difficult problems arise from a husband or wife remaining tied to his or her mother's apron strings or staying overly dependent upon his or her father. The position of the parents of married children is one of advice, not control. It is not possible for a couple to cleave together and become one until they leave their parents.

God's pattern is that they leave dependency on parents and become their own institution and cleave to each other. She must look to her husband as head, not her father or pastor or anyone else. He must look to her for intimate help and completing, not to his mother or secretary or anyone else. **God's pattern is that only the husband meet the wife's need for headship, and only the wife meet the husband's intimate needs.**

The man and his wife are to be naked before each other, and yet not embarrassed or ashamed. **Intimacy is a part of God's pattern.** One major problem in marriages is a lack of intimacy. Intimate communication is vital to any marriage relationship. There is great fulfillment in loving intimacy between a husband and wife, much the same as there is in a loving, intimate relationship between man and God. Intimacy can exist only with transparency in an atmosphere of unconditional love when both are naked and open to each other emotionally, physically, and spiritually. There can be no great secrets, no deception, no hidden agendas, no defensive walls, no whitewashed coverings, and no manipulation.

True intimacy is a deep need for every married couple. **God's pattern is that nothing exist between the couple that hinders**

their being one flesh. One must speak the truth in love. However, a husband or wife must lovingly consider how and when to reveal information that might be hard for the mate to bear.

These patterns are the same for the relationship of God and man as they are for the natural family. The wife of Christ (the purified church) must be completely open and transparent with Jesus for real intimacy to exist. As Jesus is the head of the wife (church), the husband is the head of the wife in a natural family. As Jesus is to the church so the husband is to the wife. As the church is to Jesus so the wife is to the husband.

The natural family is to be a clear picture to the world of God's relationship to His wife, the church. The husband represents Jesus who must bring life and headship to the church (the wife). The children are the fruit or the production of the marriage. They are to become the image of their father, Jesus. The husband (Jesus) is to be closely related to Father God and do and say what He sees and hears the Father doing and saying. Wives, like the church, are to greatly respect and be subject to their husbands.

Eph. 5:22-24, Amp.: ***Wives, be subject - be submissive and adapt yourselves to your own husbands*** *as a service to the Lord.* ***For the husband is the head of the wife as Christ is the Head of the church,*** *Himself the Savior of (His) body. As the church is subject to Christ, so let wives also be subject in everything to their husbands.*

To understand God's family pattern we must distinguish the difference between person and office. **Man or woman is who we are. Husband and wife are offices in which we can serve.** The directives from God regarding His kingdom family pattern define the offices and the responsibilities of the different offices in relating to God and to one another. **These offices are what we do, not**

who we are. Some perversions occur when we lose that understanding and fail to make the proper distinction between the person and the office. For example, men may begin to think of themselves as primary and women as secondary.

The office of husband in the **universal church** is Jesus. The wife is the purified Bride part of the church. The children are the church in general.

In a **local church** type organization the office of husband relates to the chief elder or pastor or whatever the chief leader person might be called. The office of wife relates to the elders, associate pastors, or whatever the second level of ministry might be called. The children relate to the congregation.

The office of husband in **business** relates to the president, entrepreneur, or chief executive officer. The office of wife relates to the second level management or mid-management or whatever they might be called. The children relate to the worker type employees.

In a national **government** the office of husband relates to the king, president or whatever the chief leader person might be called. The office of wife relates to the heads of state, or generals, or advisors, or parliament, or whatever the second level of government might be called. The children relate to the citizens.

The pattern is the same for the universal family of God or for the natural family, or for the local church, or for a kingdom business, or for governments. The basic responsibilities of the offices are the same in each case.

The office of husband is primary. The husband must be closely related to God and commune with God in such a way as to know what God is doing and saying for the family. He must go to God and get what the wife and children need to meet their needs. **The primary responsibility of the office of husband is to love the wife unconditionally as Christ loved the church.** The love which the husband must have for the wife must be unconditional. It cannot be dependent upon her performance. God Himself is the only source of unconditional love. The husband must get it from God and bring it to the wife. This will bring life to the wife and have a great effect on bringing her to purity.

The husband must also get the direction for the family from God and bring it to the wife. The husband must hear and see what God is doing and bring it to the family. The husband must also hear the appeals, petitions, or suggestions of the wife and then make a decision by seeking to represent the will of God in the matter.

Eph. 5:25-32 Amp.: ***Husbands, love your wives, as Christ loved the church and gave Himself up for her, so that He might sanctify her,*** *having cleansed her by the washing of water with the Word, that He might present the church to Himself in glorious splendor, without spot or wrinkle or any such things - that she might be holy and faultless. Even so husbands should love their wives as (being in a sense) their own bodies. He who loves his own wife loves himself. For no man ever hated his own flesh, but nourishes and carefully protects and cherishes it, as Christ does the church, because we are members of His body. For this reason a man shall leave his father and his mother and shall be joined to his wife, and the two shall become one flesh. This mystery is very great, but I speak concerning (the relation of) Christ and the church.*

The office of wife is vital and distinct in function. As the husband is the head, the wife is the heart of the family. As the seed (word, vision, or idea) comes from God through the husband it must be planted in the wife, nurtured, and developed in her before it is given birth into the world as a child.

We have seen the wife's part of being subject to and of submitting to her own husband as head -- just as the church is subject to Jesus as head. Submitting to headship is very important in God's pattern. But it is not the most important function of the office of wife toward her husband. Her most important function is the same as the husband -- that is to love God with her whole heart and relate to Him in such a way that she can have what she needs to fulfill her responsibility toward her husband. The thing that she must have is just as important to her husband as love is to the wife. But it is not love; nor is it submission. As important as those things are, they are not her number-one responsibility to her husband.

The number-one responsibility of the wife is to RESPECT her husband. This is relatively easy to do if he is bringing love to her and is perfect in all of his character. However, this respect must also be unconditional.

As unconditional love flowing from the husband ministers life to the wife, **unconditional respect** flowing from the wife ministers life to the husband. Only God can provide this kind of respect. Respect is a reflection of love. **God's pattern is that unconditional love be reflected back by the wife to the husband as unconditional respect.** This respect will go a long way toward moving the husband to perform better as a husband. It becomes a strong motivational force for him to correct flaws and to do better. Nagging, debate, and disrespect have exactly the opposite effect.

*Eph. 5:33 Amp.: However, let each man of you (without exception) love his wife as (being in a sense) his very own self; and **let the wife see that she respects and reverences her husband - that she notices him, regards him, honors him, prefers him, venerates and esteems him; and that she defers to him, praises him, and loves and admires him exceedingly.***

A Godly wife is a very valuable thing in God's creation. The wife is vital to bringing forth the will and plan of God on earth.

Without Godly wives, there will be no manifestation of the kingdom of God on earth. As it is with Jesus and the church, so it is with husband and wife.

The person in the office of wife has no more right to correct or overrule her husband than the church has to correct or overrule Jesus. But the wife has the right and the responsibility to petition or appeal to the office of husband and to make suggestions. Any attempt by the wife to usurp authority and rule over or apart from the husband will be seen as rebellion by the office of husband. Just as love from the husband ministers life to the wife and unlove from the husband ministers death to the wife, so also respect from the wife ministers life to the husband, disrespect from the wife ministers death to the husband.

The children are the fruit of the marriage -- the production of God. The office of child is a beginning office. Yet the children are being prepared to occupy the office of husband or wife as they mature. The need of the children is to be trained. God's kingdom pattern for family produces Godly children. Everything needed is provided for the children. The **primary responsibility of the children is to OBEY, honor, and esteem their parents.**

God's pattern is for the children to be **obedient** and **honor** their parents. It will be easy for children growing up in God's kingdom family pattern to know God. They see Him demonstrated in the husband/father and wife/mother. They see a clear picture of God's love in the love their father has for their mother. They are trained in how to reflect God's love as they see their mother respect and praise her husband, their father. It is easy for them to understand God's love and to know how to respond to it with loving respect and submission.

Eph. 6: 1-3: Children, ***obey*** *your parents in the Lord (as His representatives), for this is just and right.* ***Honor*** *(esteem and value* *as precious) your father and your mother; this is the first commandment with a promise: that all may be well with you, and that you may live long on the earth.*

In God's pattern, the father is responsible for training the children. Certainly the mother has a vital part in training the children. Her part is especially important to the very young. She is especially equipped to nurture them with gentleness. The father is the source of **training** and **discipline** for the children. The mother will reflect the fathers love and help to train the children as directed by the father.

Eph. 6:4: ***Fathers**, do not irritate and provoke your children to anger, do not exasperate them to resentment, but **rear them tenderly in the training and discipline and the counsel and admonition of the Lord.***

The children feel extremely secure under the care and protection of a strong, loving father and a tender, loving mother. Fathers have a strength that instills the feelings of safety in a child. That same loving firmness gives them great assurance that firm boundaries exist for their protection. Only the special strength of a father can provide the security of discipline and protection.

Remember these principles are the same for all kingdom of God government. The basics of the kingdom of God family pattern are: (1) The person God has placed in charge of an institution of family, business, church, or state is to relate closely to God in the "office of husband" and bring the unconditional love of God and headship to the second level management (the office of wife). (2) The second level management is to unconditionally respect the "office of husband". (3) The children, employees, congregation, or citizens (the office of child) are to obey, honor, and be trained by the father working with the mother.

BASILEIA LETTER
Number 21

Change And The Kingdom of God

Jesus said "repent (change) for the kingdom of God is at hand". The central message of Jesus was the kingdom of God and the need for man to change. The life changing message of Jesus is changing our world as individual lives are being changed.

Mat 4:17 From that time Jesus began to preach and to say, ***"Repent, for the kingdom of heaven is at hand."***

Multitudes of people around the world are changing. The powerful presence of God is coming forth by the Holy Spirit b ringing the very life and power of Christ to live within believers who are willing to give up their past ways and be transformed (changed). Cities are being transformed as city officials and leaders of businesses, churches, and families are being changed by the powerful presence of God.

The transformation of a city begins with the renewing of individual minds to the kingdom of God ways. The glory of God is manifesting into our world on a personal level and then on a corporate level. Individuals must remove their mask or veil and become intimate with Christ. The presence of His glory at a personal level is life changing.

Rom 12:2: And do not be conformed to this world, but ***be transformed by the renewing of your mind****, that you may prove what is that good and acceptable and perfect will of God.*

2 Cor 3:18: ***But we all, with unveiled face, beholding as in a mirror the glory of the Lord, are being transformed into the same image from glory to glory, just as by the Spirit of the Lord.***

Individuals who are being transformed are coming together in UNITY to praise, worship, and pray powerful prayers of intercession. Strongholds of evil spiritual forces that have held the people and their cities in bondage are weakening and are being destroyed as more and more people are coming into unity with the groups of worshiping intercessors.

The glory of God is released as the UNITY of praise, worship, and intimate communion with Him begins to bring forth miracles of healing and deliverance. More people are attracted to the miracles of God and many believe as they see the power of God demonstrated before them.

Deep commitment develops in the people as they are captivated by the reality of the presence and power of God. The release from darkness and the cleansing from evil brings freedom and joy. The city is transformed into righteousness, peace, and joy in the Holy Spirit. Crime goes down, domestic violence and stress at all levels are lessened, and prosperity increases in the city.

One of the many cities around the world where a documented transformation has occurred is Cali Columbia. Cali was once known as the cocaine capital of the world. Drug lords had bought up the finest mansions of the city. With their money and fear they ruled the city and much of the country. People in responsible positions of government and media who would not cooperate were murdered. The Cali cartel was said to be one of the richest, most powerful, and best organized crime organization of all time. Billions of dollars were at their disposal. Walls went up to protect the mansions of drug lords and murders were daily occurrences in the city. The drug lords not only ruled in political matters they had influence in the religious realm and participated in the occult practices that were strongly rooted in the city.

The churches were not very powerful. There was disunity among the pastors in the city -- churches were divided and each did there own thing.

Intercession made the difference. God sent a man who believed that if the church would come together in unity and pray God would change the city. They began by praying and asking God to show them how to pray. God led them to study the city and the strongholds and problems of each area and then to intercede for the specific needs of the areas. In 1995, this led to the first city wide all night prayer and worship meeting. Many opposed it but thousands came out and prayed powerfully for the city and against the strongholds of the enemy in the city. During the weekend of this first all night prayer meeting, for the first time since anyone could remember, there were no murders in the city. There was normally up to fifteen murders each day. Within ten days after the prayer meeting the drug cartel began to crumble. Soon over sixty thousand were attending worship and prayer meetings in the giant soccer stadium. In that same year the drug lords were taken down.

In the process the man of God who had been sent to bring forth the unity and prayer became a martyr. His murder led to much greater unity among what has become over two hundred pastors who united together in a covenant of unity. Today they are the backbone of the high profile prayer meetings and the miraculous transformation of the city.

Leaders in the city came to know the Lord and have given much favor to the work of God. The unsaved have found hope and are coming to the Lord in great numbers. Churches are exploding across the city and across denominational lines. One church has seven services on Sunday as thirty five thousand people attend.

The churches recognize that unity and prayer is what has allowed the mighty revival and transformation of the city. They know it is by the Spirit of God as He has come in great power among His people.

Nothing is impossible with God. This is the new thing God is doing in many communities across the world. This is the kingdom of God coming forth and changing our world.

Today the Spirit of God is moving from church to church and from community to community looking for a people who are **hungry, humble, and willing to change** to show forth His glory and establish His kingdom ways on earth. Yet again and again the mighty river and flow of the Spirit of God is turned away from churches and communities which are left to continue in their strife and division with one another. Unwilling to lay down their territorial rule and their traditions to join themselves with others in unity, prayer and worship. As the Spirit of God comes and knocks on the door bringing the gospel of the kingdom and is **not** received, the unwilling leaders are left to find fault with those whom God sends and strive against the change of God as they continue to defend their territory and the old religious ways.

2 Chr 16:9 : "For the eyes of the LORD run to and fro throughout the whole earth, to show Himself strong on behalf of those whose heart is loyal to Him. In this you have done foolishly; therefore from now on you shall have wars."

The words that Jesus spoke to the elders and chief priest in that many sinners would enter the kingdom of God before many religious leaders yet remain true. *"Assuredly, I say to you that tax collectors and harlots enter the kingdom of God before you". (Mat 21:23-32)*

Mat 7:21 "Not everyone who says to Me, 'Lord, Lord,' shall enter the kingdom of heaven, but he who does the will of My Father in heaven.
Mat 7:22 "Many will say to Me in that day, 'Lord, Lord, have we not prophesied in Your name, cast out demons in Your name, and done many wonders in Your name?'
Mat 7:23 "And then I will declare to them, 'I never knew you; depart from Me, you who practice lawlessness!'

It appears to be easier for sinners to change and enter the kingdom of God lifestyle than for some religious people to change and receive the gospel of the GLORY of Christ, the gospel of the kingdom. The traditions of the religious leaders of the first century were obviously too strong for them to be willing to change. The demons holding the immoral sinners may not be as effective in keeping people out of the kingdom as the religious demons ruling over religious systems. The powerful religious spirits of Pharisee, Jezbel, and Anti Christ and all that work with them seek to blind the minds of men to the gospel of the kingdom -- the gospel of the GLORY of Christ. They allow partial understanding of the gospel and seek to convince men that there is no more and cause them to fight against the gospel of the kingdom -- the gospel the GLORY of Christ now. They seek to prevent unity and true praise and worship of God and to replace it with an order or system with limitations and controls imposed through religious leaders. Anyone with more truth of the gospel is a threat to them

Mat 23:13 But woe unto you, scribes and Pharisees, hypocrites! for ye shut up the kingdom of heaven against men: for ye neither go in yourselves, neither suffer ye them that are entering to go in.

Everyone wants to believe that it is someone else that is affected by the attack of religious spirits and -- it is someone else suffering from spiritual blindness and -- someone else who needs to change. We all tend to believe that what we have is right and is all we need. Our eyes must be opened. If we are not getting the desired results, if our own life, our church, and our city are not being transformed and the kingdom of God is not coming forth in them now, it is a clear evidence that we ourselves need to change. The enemy is not able to overpower the works of God. It is we ourselves that are not in order. We have power over the enemy and are here for the purpose of bringing forth the kingdom of God and to rule and reign with Him. God's power and plan are not lacking. The enemy is not able to over rule God. The lack is within men. We are the ones that must change. If what we are doing is not working, if unity is not coming forth and deep intercession, praise, and worship is not coming forth in our city destroying the works of the enemy and establishing the kingdom of God, we must admit it and change.

If we are not experiencing the powerful presence of God coming forth among us and deep intercession with praise and worship bringing forth unity among believers in our area, we are probably blinded spiritually in some areas. We may be resisting change thinking that we are defending the "gospel", or our denomination, or our place of rule in the church and city. Give it up! Let God change us until we also see, in our city, unity and prayer bringing forth the gospel of the GLORY of Christ -- the fullness of the gospel of the kingdom.

The gospel of the kingdom flowing through the mighty river of God will not continue to knock on the door of your house. You can be passed by and miss the wonderful works of God. We can be like the religious people of the first century and miss entering the kingdom of God lifestyle now. We can continue thinking that it is someone else who is causing us to be in strife and causing the disunity in our church and our community. Or we can face the reality that we ourselves or in need of change, we ourselves must be transformed into the image of Christ.

Some of us have fought the same battle in different places and at different times and have blamed the world and the devil for our continued lack of the reality of the kingdom of God lifestyle and the will of God being done in our lives, our church, and our city. We must admit that it is not God or the world or the devil -- it is us that must change and become world changers. Are we the ones with veiled faces unable to see the revelation of the kingdom of God now? If we are to be transformed we must loose the veil of religion and every other hinderance to seeing Him as He is now.

2 Cor 3:18: But we all, **with unveiled face,** *beholding as in a mirror the* **glory** *of the Lord, are being* **transformed** *into the same image from* **glory to glory,** *just as by the* **Spirit** *of the Lord.*

This verse is talking about us and the therefore in the next verse tells us it is still talking about us, not lost sinners.

2 Cor 4:1 Therefore, since we have this ministry, as we have received mercy, we do not lose heart.
2 Cor 4:2 But we have renounced the **hidden things of shame,** *not* **walking in craftiness** *nor* **handling the word of God deceitfully,** *but by manifestation of the truth commending ourselves to every man's conscience in the sight of God.*

This verse implies that it is possible for us to have *hidden things of shame* and to *walk in craftiness -- handling the word of God deceitfully.*
The subject has not changed in the next verse. The verse is still speaking to us and is not just talking to sinners about the gospel of being born again. It is talking to us about the gospel of the GLORY of Christ.

2 Cor 4:3 But even if our gospel is veiled, it is veiled to those who are perishing,
2 Cor 4:4 whose minds the god of this age has blinded, who do not believe, lest the light of the **gospel of the glory of Christ,** *who is the image of God, should shine on them.*

Is it possible that the phrase *those who are perishing* does not only refer to the eternal lost but to us who are living in debate, disunity, strife, and defeat and are not seeing the kingdom of God now in our lives, churches, and cities? Are we, like the religious people of the first century the ones who have veiled faces? If we are not seeing Him and experiencing the transformation of our home, church, business, and city into the kingdom of God we may be veiled.

No longer can I look to someone or something else to justify my lack of transformation into the fullness of Christ bringing forth His kingdom in my world. Lord it is me, standing in the need of change. In this time of the new millennium there is a shift in the things of God. **There is a hunger that exceeds anything of the past.** There is a consuming fire of God within that will not be satisfied with the ways and victories of the past. There is a universal call of God going out in these days. **Deep is again calling to deep**, but in a greater way than ever known in my lifetime. I simply must have more of Him or perhaps I must have Him to have more of me. The wonderful gifts and works of the past have been and are wonderful and my heart is grateful for them but they are not enough any more. There must be a greater intimacy a greater flow of His love and power a greater means of praise and worship -- His kingdom -- His righteousness-- His Glory must be seen and experienced in my life or I cannot be satisfied.

I was privileged to live a year in a some what remote log cabin alone with the presence of God. God was with me all day every day in a special closeness. It was the high point of my life. It was hard when the Lord ended that very special season and sent me out to be with people and to share what He had given me during that wonderful time of closeness. But even that no longer seems enough. It is wonderful for Him to be where I am but something within me desires to be where He is spiritually, not just Him where I am. I must have more. I must go to a higher place with Him. I must be changed again. I know there is much that must be changed in or about me but I have no understanding as to what it is. I just know that I must not continue at the same level of bringing forth His life and kingdom into the world. The results of ministry I have seen to this point are wonderful and I truly thank Him for them, but they are not enough. I must be more transformed. I must see homes, churches, and cities transformed into the glorious kingdom of God.

I know that I am not alone in this but that God is speaking to many of His people in the same way. I know there are others with this fire in their heart that will not be quenched. I know there is a great longing to see His people changed and the great harvest come in, but there is more. It is the longing to be where He is and to know and be known of Him in even a greater depth. **It is deep calling to deep.** I know there are others He is speaking to in this way who are also in tears often as the longing for Him and the fullness of His kingdom flood and overfill our hearts.

If you are still debating religious things and striving in this life, please consider the time and the call of God to seek Him with your whole heart now -- even to the point of giving up religious rule and systems. This is the time that all of God's people who have gone before us longed to see and did not see.

Let's not miss any of what God is doing in this time. Let's allow Him to change us and to make us into world changers.

BASILEIA LETTER
Number 22

Transformation To The Kingdom of God

Jesus said that He came to fulfill the laws of God on earth -- to establish God's righteous ways of doing and being on earth as in heaven.

Mat 5:17: "Do not think that I came to destroy the Law or the Prophets. I did not come to destroy but to fulfill."

In Matthew chapters 5,6, &7 Jesus began to explain that his mission was to change the issues of the hearts of mankind to the ways of God and thereby bring forth the kingdom of God lifestyle on earth. He taught a new and living way which was greater than the old way and seemed backward to the minds of the hearers. He taught that adultery was a heart issue. He taught that murder is anger in the heart. He taught to turn the other cheek -- go the extra mile -- love your enemies -- bless those who curse you -- do good to those who hate you -- and pray for those who spitefully use you and persecute you. These and other issues of the heart fulfill the laws and plan of God on earth.

Jesus is the fulfillment of the law and plan of God. His perfect sinless life ended on earth with His crucifixion as the lamb of God to pay the full price for lawlessness (sin). Jesus rose from the dead, ascended to the Father, and then **returned in the Holy Spirit to indwell believers** and to complete the practical fulfillment of establishing God's kingdom lifestyle, first in the hearts of believers and then through them into the world, thus fulfilling the law.

*Col 1:27: To them God willed to make known what are the riches of the glory of this mystery among the Gentiles: which is **Christ in you, the hope of glory.***

*2 Cor 3:18: But we all, with unveiled face, beholding as in a mirror the glory of the Lord, are being **transformed** into the same image from glory to glory, just as **by the Spirit of the Lord**.*

A great transformation is taking place in our world. God is moving upon people -- changing lives -- changing our ways of thinking and doing -- changing communities -- changing cultures -- changing our world. The metamorphic transformation now regenerating and reforming mankind is bringing forth God's kingdom of heaven ways on earth. The old worldly ways of doing things does not fit into the design of God now being made manifest in our world. God is now bringing into view what appears to mankind to be a new thing. It is, however, not a new thing but His old thing -- the way God has intended for life to be lived on Planet Earth from its conception.

Mankind has sought diligently to govern his life on the planet apart from the design of God. The alternate plans that mankind and the devil have devised and implemented have failed to bring true righteousness, peace, and joy to the people of the world. All of the problems facing mankind have been brought about by man's abandoning God's ways and seeking other methods of governing life. Consequently all of the problems facing mankind can be potentially overcome or neutralized by mankind ordering his life by the ways of God. Through many generations the souls of mankind have been trained in systems of beliefs and practices different from those designed by God.

In recent times God is magnifying and accelerating His presence and influence upon mankind. The outpouring of the Spirit of

God is bringing renewal and revival. Lifestyles are changing as people are being drawn by the Spirit of God and are turning to His ways.

Hunger for God is motivating many people to alter their lifestyles and provide time in their schedules to seek the intimate presence of God. The religious liturgy and ritualistic practices of the past have not fed the spirits and souls of the multitudes. Men, women, teens, and children are searching for more in life than occasional breaks from their busy lifestyles of pleasure seeking for halfhearted religious church services. Hours of viewing empty and often violent and sexually laden television programming are not satisfying the hunger of the hearts of the multitudes of spiritually starving people. This great hunger across the world is growing as the malnourished heart and soul of mankind is withering for lack of virtue. Secular education has for the most part focused on self improvement to gain power and wealth and has often proven to be lacking real virtue and satisfaction in life. Sexual promiscuity and extremes of dress and social practice provide no real nourishment to the soul starved for true virtue of God.

In this scene of only virtual reality and perplexing starvation for true supernatural reality, **a bright light of virtue is now shining into our world**. Starving people are becoming desperate as the reality they have longed for is beginning to come into view. Their spiritual senses are becoming intensified and their entire beings are quickened with excitement as the spiritual aroma of real spiritual food comes to their senses.

I can still remember as a boy walking down the street on a warm evening in the old fashioned neighborhood where I grew up. Doors and windows of the houses which were only a few yards from the sidewalk were open and the smell of supper cooking drifted out into the street. I was already hungry but when the smell of frying steak or chicken and other wonderful smells met me as I passed the different houses I became desperate to get home for supper. My steps quickened into a run as excitement and anticipation tugged at my hungry body. I was filled with feelings of desperation to get home and be filled with Mom's good cooking.

The light of the presence and glory of God is now coming forth to dispel the darkness of the shadow of death from the church and the world. As people sense the supernatural presence of the Spirit of God coming forth in spots of revival here and there, their hunger is turning into deep desperation. As starved youth begin to taste the wonderful flavor of purity and holiness in the joyful presence of God they become desperate for more and desperate for others to come to the table of the Lord and be satisfied with the good food of spiritual reality. Life priorities change in view of the reality of God in their lives. Things that seemed very important become less important. Being in God's presence and serving Him becomes paramount in their lives.

Many mature or elderly people who have hungered for God and sought Him for many years are now experiencing their hunger turn into desperation as they sense the time has come of the outpouring of His Spirit. They have tasted of God's glory and must have more. The old ways of religion are crumbling and the new ways of the very presence and power of God are bringing reformation to the church. The church will never be the same again as the minds and hearts of men are being reformed by the presence of God.

Over the past four or five hundred years, **God has continued to move His church toward reformation through restoration.** Increasing parts and pieces of revelation and spiritual power have been restored to the Body of Christ through many moves of God over the past several centuries. In the past few decades, especially in the nineties, the moves of God seem to have increased in frequency and intensity. The fire of God yet continues to increase, restoring and reforming the church. Each of the previous recent moves have had, and continue to have, a distinctive part in the reformation. There is overlap in the moves and any personal need can be met by any of the current moves of God. Needs such as salvation, baptism of the Spirit, healing, deliverance, can all be met. Yet, each move can be identified as having an emphasis on one phase of ministry or reformation.

As an example some of the recent moves of God in the nineties can be easily traced to **Argentina**. **The great revival in Argentina emphasized supernatural power evangelism and deliverance.** The fire spread from Argentina to other spots in the world including a very significant outpouring in **Toronto**, Canada. **The emphasis in Toronto became the love of Father God bringing emotional and physical healing.** In Toronto prideful religious views were washed away along with past wounds as the pure love of God flooded souls and overcame diseases of soul and body. From Toronto many fires were spread around the world including a very significant one in **Pensacola**, Florida. **The emphasis in Pensacola became repentance and cleansing from sin as hundreds of thousands over a period of years rushed to the alters to repent and be purged.** And from Pensacola the fire spread to many other places including another very significant outpouring in the tiny town of **Smithton**, Missouri. **The emphasis in Smithton is the reformation of the church to the kingdom of God.** The move of God that began in Smithton, Missouri and has now moved to Kansas City, Missouri and is now becoming known as the "Smithton Outpouring of Kansas City" or "World Revival Church of Kansas City" is a significant next step in the ongoing revelation of God and reformation of the church. Thousands of pastors have been changed and many have taken the fire of revival back to their own churches. Over a quarter million people (250,000) from every state and over fifty nations have made the trip to Smithton seeking to be changed in the presence of God.

BASILEIA LETTER
Number 22

On March 24th of 1996 a bolt of spiritual fire like lightening suddenly hit **Pastor Steve Gray** and the Smithton Community Church in the tiny Missouri farm town of Smithton and a future world move of God was planted as a seed from God into the rich soil of the desperate hunger of Steve Gray. Over the next four years the seed sprouted and grew and World Revival Church of Kansas City was birthed after multitudes of people were touched and changed by the powerful presence of God at Smithton.

Steve and Kathy Gray along with the other servants of God who have been a part of helping birth this move of God are all just ordinary humble folks who have been touched by the fire of God and become extraordinary in their commitment to the work of revival. The level of commitment and loyalty of these people is extreme and is only exceeded by the vigorous life pouring forth from them. Those who stay don't seem to miss the natural worldly activities they no longer have time for in the outpouring of the Spirit of God. Everyone moves together as a team in attending the five services each week and serving the many guest who come to be changed. Everyone seems to some degree to recognize that this is an apostolic work brought forth by God to impact the church and the world with true reformation and they are more than willing to sacrifice personally to continue to be a part of the outpouring of God.

Some people have had difficulty understanding the intense commitment and loyalty of the Grays and those serving in this move of God. There are different callings and different places of service in the body of Christ. The apostolic type of work necessary to bring forth this awesome move that is touching the world is quite different from pastoring and teaching in a local church. The intensity and level of commitment required is different.

One can be a pastor who receives of the movement and then uses the reformed ways of God to serve his local body of believers.

Or in some other way one can continue to serve the Lord on a more local basis of meeting the needs of people and seeking to transform one's community to the ways of God. But, if a person decides to be a directly connected part of an apostolic movement like the World Revival Church of Kansas City, the level of commitment will be extreme. Can you imagine the amount of time and effort Paul and the other apostles spent during the transitional time of the first century outpouring of the Spirit of God. Even Jesus and the disciples with Him at times did not have time to eat and have normal rest.

Many other significant outpourings of God's Spirit have occurred and are yet occurring, not only in local churches but also in great itinerate ministries. These apostolic itinerate ministries also each bring forth different emphases, but by the same Spirit they are all bringing revival. For example, God has sent men like **Rodney Howard-Brown** with an emphasis of the joy of the Lord and the freedom it produces. Through Rodney God brought a demonstration of the power and joy of God and enlightenment exposing man made religion as an empty shell laced with doctrines of demons. Through another great evangelist, **Reinhard Bonnke**, God is bringing the salvation of cities as millions are coming together for gigantic open air meetings in Africa. In these unprecedented meetings hundreds of thousands are coming to Christ and multitudes of miracles and healings are taking place.

All of the men leading the powerful apostolic type ministries bringing forth reformation would probably have similar stories of becoming so hungry for God that they became desperate. **Steve Gray** says that he believes that for an instant in time he became the most desperate man in the world and God responded. He was so intensely desperate for the outpouring of God upon himself and his church that nothing else mattered and he could not go on. He refused to return to church and try to go on without revival. When he became intensely desperate God showed up in a lightening like bolt of spiritual power and neither he nor his church has ever been the same again. Rodney Howard-Brown became so desperate that he told God, "God, you either come down here tonight and touch me, or I'm going to die and come up there and touch you." He frightened everyone around as he shouted for twenty minutes, "GOD I WANT YOUR FIRE!" He got what he cried out for in desperation. The world is yet being changed by ordinary men like these who reached a level beyond hunger for God and became desperate.

In the **Smithton Outpouring of Kansas City**, God has sent a move of real life purity, holiness, and power upon the earth bringing the seeds of the kingdom of God lifestyle to reform the church and change the world. The coming together of the fire of revival and the Word of the kingdom is being brought with clarity and power to believers and church leaders around the world. The Smithton outpouring is a balance of the miracle working, soul saving, delivering and healing power manifestations of God and a pure revelation and scholarly presentation of the living Word of God. Steve's preaching is well received and seems to be infused directly into the hearts of the people in the presence of God. Steve always has a fresh word from God and almost never repeats a message. The Smithton Outpouring is at this moment in time the next move of God and is truly planting the seeds of the kingdom of God lifestyle and bringing reformation to the church.

It seems that God has brought a balance of the previous emphases together in the Smithton Outpouring. There is the powerful manifestations of the Spirit but they are not the emphasis. There is the powerful Word preached and taught but that is not the emphasis. There is powerful prayer, salvation, filling of the Spirit, physical healing, miracles, emotional healing, deliverance, strengthening of families, restoration of pastors and leaders, prophesy and other gifts but none of these things are the emphasis of this powerful balanced move of the in-breaking kingdom of God in the

Smithton Outpouring. The church in general is not preached as right and all the rest of the world free game for bashing from the pulpit. Purity and holiness are practical and real goals and the preaching does not consist of bashing the lost and sinful people of the world. Rather the church is seen as the focus for revival, and when revived, the church will bring forth real change to the hearts and lives of the needy people of the world. The emphasis at the **World Revival Church in Kansas City and the World Revival Network is the revival and reformation of the worldwide church.** The world has only begun to taste the in-breaking kingdom of God flowing through this ministry. The impact of the kingdom lifestyle is destined to affect the world. **As powerful revival continues by the outpouring of God's Spirit through this and other ministries the church is being reformed and the whole world will never be the same again.**

Those seeking to live God's way must be reformed -- their souls must be retrained in the goals and ways of God's kingdom. Man must have new purposes in life and new ways of living. The principles of God's kingdom are redefining what life is about -- how to do business God's way -- how to have successful marriages -- how to rear godly children -- how to have a powerful church or ministry -- how to have peace and goodwill on earth.

Love is the greatest principle in the kingdom of God.

The pure love of God flowing from God through the Spirit of Christ within man, is first reflected back to God and then also flows out to our neighbor bringing the fulfillment of the law of God on earth. Because of this love, man is motivated and restrained to **obedience toward God and to goodwill toward mankind.**

Matthew 22:36-40: "*Teacher, which is the* **great commandment** *in the law?" Jesus said to him,* "***You shall love the Lord your God with all your heart, with all your soul, and with all your mind.*** *This is the first and great commandment. And the second is like it:* ***You shall love your neighbor as yourself.*** *On these two commandments hang all the Law and the Prophets.*"

True prosperity in every area of life is the natural result of walking in the love of God. God's love purifies mankind and changes his focus from himself to God and others. The person walking in this love no longer thinks first of himself and his need and how to get more of what he wants. The thoughts of his heart become, how can I serve God? -- how can I help meet the needs of others?

Seeking to serve leads to increased **production** as goods and services are needed to meet the practical and spiritual needs of others. One thinks, "how can I use what I have to establish systems and ways to meet the needs of others". **Business** is born and will be diligently brought forth as the principle of **heartiness** is evident in a heart felt work based on the love of God instead of greed and meeting one's own need. **Diligence** and **heartiness** in productive activity are normal results of God's love in us seeking to meet others needs.

The major kingdom principle of **LOVE** begins to bring forth many other lessor kingdom principles. We can identify the principles of **purification, prosperity, serving, heartiness, diligence,** and many others which flow from love.

The great universal kingdom law of **sowing and reaping** causes increased prosperity as we continue to increase service to others. Even the second greatest kingdom principle, **FAITH**, works through love. As God's purification, and plan flows through us, it becomes easy to believe God. It becomes easy to trust Him for greater things as we experience His blessing flowing through us in the production which He has put into our hearts to meet the needs of others.

Good balance of **management practices** (or **stewardship** to use a Biblical word) flows from love as we seek to not waste and to make best use of the provisions we have in meeting the needs of others. We are restrained from selfishly consuming the resources of time, energy, money, goods, and whatever else God has placed in our hands.

HOPE, the third greatest kingdom principle is birthed through the works of love and faith. We no longer live in a hopeless world filled with depression and no visible way to escape the doom and gloom of darkness. Hope is the positive, peaceful, joyful attitude of those who are trusting in God and serving Him by serving others.

These principles begin to produce **peace** and **joy** in the life which further lifts the spirits to higher levels of life and achievement (**promotion**) in the production of life. All these things working together begin to affect the **mental and physical health** of the one flowing in the love of God. Less time and money must be directed toward cures and recovery from disease, illnesses, and addictions of every sort. This results in less loss and more production of life.

A sense of **significance of life** develops from the God directed activities of meeting the needs of others. Life becomes exciting and we become enthusiastic through significant service. **Boredom is an impossibility for those actively serving God by serving others.** There is no need for time and money to be spent on costly entertainment and activities to fill an empty life, if the life is filled with the purposes of God. Again, this means more profit.

Loving our neighbor as ourselves fosters the principle of **agreement**. One becomes agreeable instead of disagreeable. Seeking to agree rather than seeking to dominate by proving ourselves always right, brings forth **submission** to one another and stops strife and disputes which lead to decreased production.

Christ is the very essence of kingdom principles. As His presence in-dwells us by the Holy Spirit, great increase of life is produced -- a true abundance of life. All of this leaves no room for lingering pain from past wounds nor resentment in any form. Thus our lives are healed and free of lingering pain. There is no need for emotional pain killers of alcohol and drug abuse or self administered pity to try to attract the attention of others to help us with our painful life experience. **FREEDOM** from all bondages is the natural result of the presence of God in one's life. And again, the great cost of these bondages is saved and profitable production is increased.

Kingdom of God principles lead to quality life decisions.

Walking in the Spirit and living in the kingdom of God lifestyle leads us to make decisions that will be most profitable for life. Relating to the Spirit of God within causes us to have His desires placed into our heart. We can then follow the desires of our heart into significant and productive life. Our hearts desire from God becomes the place of our greatest gifting and blessing.

BASILEIA LETTER

Number 23

Power In The Kingdom of God

Jesus said, *"**you shall receive power** when the Holy Spirit has come upon you." (Acts 1:8)*

--- Luke 24:49: *"Behold, I send the Promise of My Father upon you; but tarry in the city of Jerusalem until you are **endued with power from on high**."*

-- 1 Cor 4:20: For the **kingdom of God is not in word but in power**.

How much and what kind of power were the disciples to receive?

What is the purpose of this power from heaven?

Does anyone have this power from heaven now?

Can we have this power now? If so, how do we get it?

Do you want more power from on high in your life?

If so, why do you want it? How much do you want it?

The Greek word translated power in the above verses is **"dunamis"**, and is defined in the Strongs Greek Dictionary as: "G1411. dunamis, doo'-nam-is; from G1410; **force** (lit. or fig.); spec. **miraculous power** (usually by impl. **a miracle itself**):--ability, abundance, meaning, might (-ily, -y, -y deed), **(worker of) miracle (-s)**, power, strength, violence, mighty (wonderful) work."

The power the disciples were to receive and the power of the kingdom of God is **a force of mighty miracle working strength -- a force from heaven that is beyond the natural -- a supernatural miraculous power.**

God Himself is the source of this power. The power that spoke all things into being and continues to cause all things to exist and consist -- the power that raised Christ Jesus from the dead is now potentially available in mankind. There are those who have tapped into the unlimited power of Almighty God. They have somehow entered into the realm of the supernatural miracle working power of God in this life now.

Barbara and I have chosen as God has directed us to invest our lives in being a part of the revival of power and presence of God in our world today. The more we spend time in the places where God is moving and with the men and women God is using to demonstrate His miracle working power, the more hungry we become for the powerful presence of God to bring forth great changes in our world -- to bring forth the kingdom of God destroying wickedness and establishing righteousness. The more we see wrecked lives renewed and changed -- people healed, delivered, set free and filled with joy, the more we desire Him.

One of God's chosen and anointed servants who is making a powerful difference, especially among the youth, is Bob Bradbury. Bob was a fisherman from Galilee, Rhode Island USA when at fifty plus years of age God and Randy Clark got hold of him in the early days of the great outpouring in Toronto, Canada. Soon Bob had sold his sea going fishing boat, airplane, boat building business and whatever else to pour out the power anointing God has graced him with.

Young people that range from street wise gang members to backslidden church kids are instantly changed as they encounter the power (dunamis) of God flowing through Bob. Preschool children, college students, and drop outs are all equally affected and changed by a power encounter as Bob simply tells them God loves them and wants to use them to change the world. He invites them to come and get a touch from God. The unsaved, backslidden, half hearted believers, and sincere believers all alike are powerfully touched as he prays for them or has some of the youth who have already received an impartation to pray for them.

In one of Bob's meetings, a weeping mother calls out to Bob from the congregation, "My fifteen year old daughter has strayed from God. I have prayed for eleven months and she only gets worse. What can I do." Bob replies, "Just get her here and the power of God will do the rest." In one evening the rebellious teen is transformed by the power of God as Bob gently lays hands on her and prays for her and invites other teens who have already been transformed to pray for her. The girls eyes fill with tears and she is obviously overwhelmed by the (dunamis) power of God. After a time on the floor being ministered to by the Holy Spirit her heart and life is transformed. Before the evening is over Bob instructs her in praying for others who have come for ministry and the power of God moves through her as even the adults fall under the power of God and receive from the Holy Spirit. Multiply this true story by thousands and you have some idea of what God is doing through one man. Then multiply it again by thousands and you will have an idea of what God is doing through thousands of people to change our world in this day. Cities are being transformed and nations are being affected by the power of God flowing through ordinary people who have received the authority of Christ to flow the power of God to other ordinary people who are hungry for more of God.

There is a season of God coming upon the earth in which many will come into the glorious reality of a relationship with God that will allow a release of the miracle working power (dunamis) of God into the world on an unprecedented scale. Never before has the world seen the awesome release of the mature sons of God walking in His supernatural power on such a large scale. Works of God that exceed the works of Jesus and the disciples in the first century will come forth on the earth as the conditions are met by the sons of God to receive the authority to flow the power of God. God greatly desires to release His power from heaven on earth through many sons. (Rom 8:19) (Heb 2:10)

God's purpose for releasing His power in mankind is the redemption of the world. The salvation of man for heaven after death is a part of that redemption, but God's purpose is larger and more comprehensive. **God's purpose in releasing power from heaven is to bring forth the kingdom of heaven on earth as it is in heaven.**

The unlimited power of God is potentially available to change the world with and through mankind. The entire planet can be changed from the ways of men and the devil to the holy ways of God. The sin of man can be wiped from the face of the earth and the glory of God established in every area of life on the planet. The power of the Creator is available to work with and through mankind to create the kingdom of heaven on earth. What will it take for this power to be flowing in your life?

Man must have specific authority from God to use the force or power of God in the world. Great **power** must always be accompanied by great **authority**. To be safe and effective, power must be restrained and focussed. Power must be released in the right place at the right time at the correct rate. It must be directed toward the target and restrained from other non target areas.

Another Greek word sometimes translated "power" in the New Testament is **"exousia"** and means primarily **"authority"**. It is defined as follows: G1849. exousia, ex-oo-see'-ah; from G1832 (in the sense of ability); **privilege**, i.e. (subj.) force, capacity, **competency**, freedom, or (obj.) **mastery** (concr. magistrate, superhuman, potentate, token of control), **delegated influence:--authority**, jurisdiction, liberty, power, right, strength.

Man must receive the authority (exousia) from God to use the miraculous power (dunamis) from God. There are conditions that must be met in the heart and life before these power gifts from God can be received by man. Many Christians seem to think that just because they are of the Christian faith they have power and authority over the devils and things of the world. Yet many continue to be plagued with demonic oppression and disorders in their lives and are unable to be a substantial factor in overcoming evil in the world. Many who seek to minister continue to find their efforts produce little or no real fruit and long for the power to make real change in peoples lives and subsequently the world.

All power and authority is given unto Jesus. (Mat 28:18) Only Jesus can give the miracle working power and authority of God to man.

*Luke 9:1 Then he called his twelve disciples together, and gave them **power** and **authority** over all devils, and to cure diseases.*

Later Jesus sent out seventy others and gave them power and authority over evil spirits and disease. Jesus often demonstrated power and authority over all the works of the enemy and over all nature. But only on a few occasions did He share that power with a few selected people. (Luke 10:1)

Before Jesus' crucifixion He promised that many would be given the power and authority to do the works that He did and even greater works.

John 14:12: "*Most assuredly, I say to you, he who believes in Me, **the works that I do he will do also; and greater works than these** he will do, because I go to My Father.*

At Jesus' resurrection and ascension the miracle working power of God, which was on the earth in Jesus, left the earth with Him. It was necessary for the disciples to wait in Jerusalem for the return of the power (dunamis) of God in Jesus by the Holy Spirit to in-dwell believers. At Pentecost the awesome power of God returned to earth and in-dwelled those believers who were chosen to be filled with miracle working power and given authority to change the world by overcoming the works of the enemy and establishing the ways and works of God.

These began immediately to speak by the Spirit with authority and began to manifest astonishing demonstrations of the Spirit . Their teaching and preaching became like Jesus with authority and demonstration of miracle working power. The people had been astonished when the power of God was evident in Jesus as he spoke with authority and power and cast out unclean spirits. Now they were seeing that same authority and power in these disciples.

*Luke 4:31-36: Then He went down to Capernaum, a city of Galilee, and was teaching them on the Sabbaths. And they were astonished at His teaching, for His word was with **authority**.*

Now in the synagogue there was a man who had a spirit of an unclean demon. And he cried out with a loud voice, saying, "Let us alone! What have we to do with You, Jesus of Nazareth? Did You come to destroy us? I know who You are; the Holy One of God!"

But Jesus rebuked him, saying, "Be quiet, and come out of him!" And when the demon had thrown him in their midst, it came out of him and did not hurt him.

> *Then they were all amazed and spoke among themselves, saying, "What a word this is! For with **authority** and **power** He commands the unclean spirits, and they come out."*

Why did Jesus choose to give this power and authority to only a select few during His life on earth and why did He through the Holy Spirit come first only to those waiting in the upper room?

Why is it today that some are seeing these great miracles in their life and ministry and some are not? In these days of revival, more people are being chosen to receive authority to demonstrate the miracle working power of God. Yet there are others who call themselves believers who are not receiving it? What makes the difference in one who only wishes for the miracle working power of God to flow in and through their lives and those who actually see the miracle working power of God working through their lives?

Perhaps, the real question for you and me is: **How can I obtain the authority (exousia) to have the power (dunamis) of God flow through me?**

We don't need more theological discussions or religious formulas about this. We must have what the twelve and the seventy received from Jesus. We must have what Bob Bradbury and many others have in their lives today. What makes them different? How are they different from many others who wish they had the power of God and who seek it and may even try to act as though they have it, but do not have the reality of the power of God flowing through their lives?

How and why did these receive the impartation of the power of God? How can we receive the impartation of the power of God?

There may not be a simple one, two, three answer to these all important questions, but perhaps we can get some help from a brief look at some characteristics of those walking in (dunamis) power.

One thing that sticks out is that the twelve and the seventy had all been with Jesus. They had sold out and given up other things in life to just be with Jesus -- to walk with Him and be a part of what He was doing. Jesus is the anointed one and the anointing of power flows through Him. He is the one in authority and is the one who can impart that authority. The word in the Bible translated anointing means to be rubbed on with oil. Those who were close to Jesus were the ones who received. Those who were not close and were busy about other things in life did not receive the transference of authority and power.

The men and women of today who are demonstrating the power of God on a consistent basis and have authority to carry and impart the power of God all have sold out other things in life to focus on the one thing of being with Jesus. Often they have spent time with other men and women in whom the authority and power of God are present. The gifts and anointing are often transferred by the laying of hands by those who are anointed with Christ and filled with His power.

Only those who have been given the **authority** from Christ to receive the gifts and power will receive from the laying on of hands -- those with whom He has been intimate -- who have proven themselves trustworthy and have a pure heart and no other gods in their lives. God will not allow the authority to remain for an extended time on those whom He does not know and trust.

A touch from God is not the same as impartation. A touch can prepare one to give their life to God. But an impartation is for those who have figuratively sold all and can now be trusted with the awesome power of God. They will use what they are given only according to the desire of God. There are no other needs or priorities that drive them. Obedience to the Spirit of God is essential to walking in power. God will not release true spiritual authority to those who are not walking in obedience.

No amount of money or sacrifice can purchase the power of God for a believer with impurities yet existing in the heart. The wounded and yet unhealed heart containing any amount of resentment or bitterness in any form cannot obtain the authority of Christ to flow the power of God.

Acts 8:18-23: And when Simon saw that through the laying on of the apostles' hands the Holy Spirit was given, he offered them money, saying, "Give me this power also, that anyone on whom I lay hands may receive the Holy Spirit."

But Peter said to him, "Your money perish with you, because you thought that the gift of God could be purchased with money! ***"You have neither part nor portion in this matter, for your heart is not right in the sight of God.***

*"Repent therefore of this your wickedness, and pray God if perhaps the thought of your heart may be forgiven you. "For I see that you are **poisoned by bitterness and bound by iniquity."***

The authority and power of God is only in God. God desires to in-dwell believers and to demonstrate His power and authority through us. Yet, He is a holy God and cannot dwell with iniquity. True inner holiness in our hearts is the only place for God to dwell and to rest His authority and power. Sometimes the road of purification to holiness can take one through much **repentance and brokenness**. Only our love for God and our sincere desire for Him can bring us through deep purification. Seeking Him with our whole heart will bring us into a relationship with Him that allows His life and power to flow through us.

BASILEIA LETTER
Number 24

Waiting And Listening For The Kingdom of God

Jesus did not say to the disciples, "Just show up at the next meeting." He said, **"Follow Me."**

He went to people who were busy doing other things and gave them promises and instructions like, **"Follow Me** and I will make you fishers of men -- go and sell what you have, give to the poor and **follow Me** -- let the dead bury the dead, come and **follow Me** -- deny yourself, take up your cross and **follow Me**". Jesus meant for the disciples then and the disciples of today to be with Him -- learn from watching Him and listening to Him -- do as He does and be as He is all day every day, not just show up at meetings. Jesus intends for all to be active in ministry (serving/waiting) in the kingdom of God. He desires for all to have an intimate relationship with Him -- to hear His voice and commune with Him.

One of the ploys of the enemy working through religious teachings of the passing church emphasis age has been to cause the people of the church to think they were supposed to sit in a pew and wait for the kingdom of God. Many have been seduced into believing that their responsibility toward the kingdom of God is to show up for meetings and watch the clergy do the "religious stuff". Jesus hates the doctrine of the Nicolaitans which divided the people into clergy and laity and separated the laity from spiritual life and responsibility except to pay tithes, and attend services.

Rev 2:6: "But this you have, that you hate the deeds of the Nicolaitans, which I also hate.

The people of the kingdom emphasis age today are understanding that waiting for the kingdom of God is much more than passively sitting in a church building. The writers of the New Testament who were passionately giving their lives for the kingdom of God never intended to imply that people should idly wait for the kingdom. The words they used which have been translated "wait" or "waiting" in the New Testament are not words of idle inactivity. The Greek words have meanings of serving, ministering, personal intimacy, and constant diligence.

*Mark 15:43: Joseph of Arimathea, a prominent council member, who was himself **waiting for the kingdom of God**, coming and taking courage, went in to Pilate and asked for the body of Jesus.*

Joseph of Arimathea was busy about the kingdom of God and even taking some risk in going to Pilate and asking for the body of Jesus. The Greek word in this verse translated "waiting" is "prosdechomai".

*Strongs Greek Dictionary: G4327. prosdechomai, pros-dekh'-om-ahee; from G4314 and G1209; to admit (**to intercourse, hospitality, credence** or [fig.] **endurance**); by impl. to await (with confidence or patience):--accept, allow, look (wait) for, take.*

Another word translated "wait" in the New Testament is "proskartereo" and means to be earnestly constantly diligently attending and adhering closely to a person place or thing in service -- to persevere and be instant in service.

*Strongs Greek Dictionary: G4342. proskartereo, pros-kar-ter-eh'-o; from G4314 and G2594; **to be earnest towards**, i.e. (to a thing) **to persevere, be constantly diligent**, or (in a place) **to attend assiduously all the exercises**, or (to a person) **to adhere closely to (as a servitor)**:--attend (give self) continually (upon), continue (in, instant in, with), wait on (continually).*

Waiting for the kingdom of God means diligently serving much like a waiter waiting tables in a fine restaurant. It means serving the King by attentively listening for His request or instruction and quickly obeying His voice. A good waiter will not be distracted by other things but will have his ear tuned to hear the one whom he serves in readiness to respond. Serving in the kingdom means serving the Lord personally in praise and worship and indirectly by serving others in whom He dwells by the Spirit. *(Mat 25:40)*

The increased vigorous life coming forth in revival is causing increased activity of service to God and to His people. **Waiting and listening** for the kingdom of God is hearing and obeying God and is changing the church and eventually the world.

Spiritual revival leads to kingdom truth.

The awakening of the sleeping church is jolting many from their pews and into action worshiping, praising, praying, and serving God with dynamic energy. The great revivals of today are establishing the reality of life in God as His presence is again filling His temple — the hearts and lives of "ordinary" believers. Revived believers are actively pursuing God and His kingdom. Those seeking the kingdom of God lifestyle are no longer satisfied to give ten percent of their money and even a smaller percentage of their time and call it serving God.

Only serving Him with their whole heart — with their whole life can bring satisfaction to the revived children of God. The powerful presence of God has put a fire of desire within them that cannot be satisfied by idly watching and passively waiting. **The church watchers have become God chasers and cannot be stopped.** The reality of seeking first the kingdom of God has come into our world through revival.

The doctrine of the Nicolaitans is finally being destroyed. **Religion's invention of dividing the Body of Christ into clergy and laity is beginning to be dissolved.** The kingdom truth of the five fold ministry gifts of apostles, prophets, evangelist, pastors, and teachers in "ordinary" believers is coming forth by the Spirit in revival. Christ Jesus is beginning to be honored as head of the church in a practical real way. **The revolutionary reformation of church government has begun.**

The burden of headship that has been usurped by men and denominations is being returned to the shoulder of Christ. The body of Christ has greatly suffered for centuries as the people in the pew have been trained to reverence men as heads and depend on them for spiritual works and church government. Not only have the people failed to develop spiritual gifts and function but the "Reverends" have suffered under the undue burden of invalid headship.

The great overburden placed upon "men of the clergy" is being lifted in revival. No longer shall the weight of the congregation be on the back of the sacrificed life of the "Reverend — Minister — Pastor — Priest" or whatever title used for the paid minister — paid to do what God is now raising up a generation of willing volunteers to do in revival.

The overburden has destroyed many men who sought to fulfill a role as head of the church that God never intended. Not only has the burden been great but the temptation has also been great. Many have succumbed to the temptations and taken advantage of the undue worshipful reverence and respect of the people toward them as "heads of the church". The elevation of "clergymen" set them apart as virtual gods and not mere men. The intense affection for Christ that should have been focused on Jesus as true head of the church has been, in part, focused on "clergymen". It has been much too easy for men to become victims of the gifts and offerings of the people and begin to receive illicit affection and money to themselves. **Scandal, burnout, and failure became common terms relating to "clergymen" in the passing church emphasis age.**

Before the present day outpouring of the presence and power of God began to bring reformation, church leaders struggled with decisions. They often resorted to their own minds which were trained by seminarians in what they could intellectually glean from the Word. For centuries church "heads" and boards of deacons, elders, and denominational bosses have struggled, debated, and voted to make decisions for the church. **The reformed men and women of God are learning to listen for and hear God to receive what Christ has already decided and then represent that into the church.** Thus the burden of headship is being restored to the shoulder of Christ.

Isa 9:6: For unto us a Child is born, Unto us a Son is given; ***And the government will be upon His shoulder.*** *And His name will be called Wonderful, Counselor, Mighty God, Everlasting Father, Prince of Peace.*

Isa 9:7: Of the increase of His government and peace There will be no end, Upon the throne of David and over His kingdom, To order it and establish it with judgment and justice From that time forward, even forever. ***The zeal of the LORD of hosts will perform this.***

In a practical and real way, revival is bringing reformation. The good news is that believers, church governments, and eventually the world will be reformed to kingdom of God ways. The bad news is that **much of the old must be uprooted, torn down, destroyed and overthrown before the new can be built and planted back.**

As in the days Jeremiah it is the zeal of the Lord that is performing the reformation from government by men to the government of God — the kingdom of God. In Jeremiah Chapter One, Israel had forsaken God for other gods and established ways that had to be torn down and destroyed before God's ways could be replanted. There is a parallel in the church. In practice if not in theology other gods have ruled in the church.

*Jer 1:10 NIV: See, today I appoint you over nations and kingdoms to **uproot and tear down, to destroy and overthrow**, to build and to plant."*

The tearing down of the old can be a difficult and painful experience. The past is filled with fond memories of church experiences. Many Christian's faith seems anchored in the relics of the beautiful church buildings and the security of the familiar traditions and fond memories of the past. The future can seem very unsure when the past monuments of beliefs and systems began to crumble and burn.

I remember weeping openly recently as I watched a news video from Virginia. The video was of a beautiful one hundred and sixty two year old church building burning. Fire fighters could do little as the fire destroyed the historical landmark. As I watched the flames swirl up the tall stately steeple that had stood over the city pointing toward the heavens for generations, I felt great sadness and a painful sense of loss. I was impressed in my spirit that this is how many will feel as the old ways of religion are uprooted, torn down, destroyed, and overthrown. These same painful feelings will bruise them as they experience the old ways of the organized church being destroyed to make room for the planting of the kingdom of God ways and the building of the glorious "Bride Church".

Jer 31:28 Just as I watched over them to uproot and tear down, and to overthrow, destroy and bring disaster, so I will watch over them to build and to plant," declares the LORD.

As the children of Israel in the wilderness were unwilling to cross over and take the promised land, there will be those who will not make the transition to the glorious church. They will live and die unchanged retaining their old ways. While their children — the next generation will enter into the glorious revival of the presence of God and the extreme worship in the glorious church.
    Who are the people of God that are crossing over into the promised land of the kingdom of heaven on earth? What are they like and what is their church and lifestyle like? Who are these people who are actively waiting upon the kingdom of God and listening for the sound of His voice -- these who will not move without the direction of the voice of their God?
    They are those who move in unison together as a mighty army -- an army that remains in rank and file and never oversteps or sidesteps the will of their God. **A mighty army of "ordinary" believers filled with an extraordinary obsession for God** -- those obsessed beyond all reason with the very love of their God. Those in whom there remains no place for the devil to lay his hand or attach his hooks. A people without the religious bondages and prideful self righteousness of the past church age. A people who do not care any more about things that were once important but cares with their whole heart and life about the things of their God. A people who are dangerous because of their simple and real love that flows into and through them to the world. A people who forever will cling to the promises of their God and gladly give their lives to be in His presence and to serve Him with all their heart and strength.
    These are the people of God coming forth into our world. They are the rulers, the workers, the teachers, the moms and dads, the

soldiers from five star generals to buck privates who are one and the same unto their God. They will not rule as lord over one another but will serve one another as Lord. They are the scientist, the plumbers, the builders, and the farmers, they are the worshipers of God doing the work of God on earth. Anointed by His Spirit and filled with undeniable power and strength to do all the will of God.

The sons of the kingdom are with us now and shall continue to grow in numbers as the mighty revival of God planted by the fathers of our past and bathed in the blood of martyrs to our Lord shall cover the earth. From ocean to ocean and from mountain to mountain there shall be none who do not know of the glory of our Lord. The beginning is past and the work lies ahead of us and anyone having put their hand to this plow shall not turn back. The plowing must continue but the planting has already begun. The mighty revival of the presence and power of God shall sweep the whole earth and the planet and all of its people shall never be the same again. The harvest is upon us and shall not be stopped. At the same time the plower is plowing and the sower is sowing and the harvester is harvesting. (Amos 9:13)

What are these people like? They are like Christ Jesus. They are in fact those in whom Christ dwells bringing forth different aspects of His very life in different individuals - the possessors of differing parts of Christ who all coming together to form the whole body of Christ covering the earth. They are the risen Christ dwelling on earth to rule and reign as priest and kings. They are the physical embodiment of the glory of God. The "Christ in you the hope of glory" has become Christ living in many by the Spirit of Christ the manifest presence of the glory of God.

No earthly government or institution shall rule over the glory of God. The kingdom people will be led by Spirit appointed elders in local groups. The elders will be the loving authority to govern the local people of God. No longer will the church be a building made with hands. The local church will meet from day to day in houses or business places or great outdoor stadiums or wherever. Some elders will be gifted pastors tending the sheep. Others will be gifted teachers teaching the children young and old. And others will be evangelist reaching out to the local community harvesting their part of the world.

The apostolic government of God will be fluid and mobile. The powerfully gifted apostles and prophets will move from place to place bringing the wisdom and specific word of God for every need and in every situation. There will no longer be a "headquarters". The "quarters of the head" are in heaven and not on earth. God's chosen servant leaders will look toward the true headquarters in heaven and receive their direction for governing from the Spirit of Christ.

The apostles will receive direction for the overall body and the governing of the overall church will be in them. The prophet will receive the word for more specific an personal direction and correction.

The local elders will receive direction for the local group of believers and will know how to pastor, teach, and evangelize their areas. The elders will know which apostles to call for and when to call for them to come and bring light and government to their group. The apostles will have direction from God in agreement to go where the elders call them. If the elders should falter and need help, an apostle and/or prophet will be sent by God to bring authority and recovery to the situation.

BASILEIA LETTER
Number 25

Awakening of The Kingdom of God

Is there spiritual awakening in our world today?

Most of us tend to accept what we see around us in our local setting and what we see on the news as the way things are everywhere. And it may appear from what we see on TV, and in our local setting, that evil is abounding and God is not doing much about it.

Unfortunately, the TV news media does not do a very good job of reporting what God is doing in our world. You will hear and see about wars and evil works of men and nations from around the world. But mighty moves of God, such as thousands coming to Christ and awesome works of God that may affect entire cities and even nations will not be on your local news tonight.

Have we allowed the news media to be our primary source of spiritual awareness of the world?

Are we, like the Pharisees of the first century? Who in the day that Jesus Christ taught and preached the gospel of the kingdom, totally missed it. The great events and miracles taking place around them were seen as something other than the Son of God proclaiming the kingdom of God. Many people who lived at the same time and in the same place where the mighty works of God were taking place, were not aware of what was occurring. Religious leaders of that day were convinced that Jesus was not doing things the right way and that His doctrine was wrong.

Is it possible that Jesus is doing more in the world today than we know about? Is it possible that we are in danger of missing some great works Jesus is doing through the Holy Spirit in awakenings and outpourings in our world today?

There have been reports of many major outpourings and revivals in recent years and in past centuries in the USA and other parts of the world.

The outpouring of the Holy Spirit brought revival among the **American colonies** in 1734-5. Over 50,000 were converted. Jonathan Edwards described the characteristics of that move as, first, an extraordinary sense of the awful majesty, greatness, and holiness of God, and second, a great longing for humility before God and adoration of God.

In 1739 there were astonishing moves of God in **England.** The Wesleys and Whitefield along with about 60 others held a prayer meeting in London. The Spirit of God moved powerfully on them all. Many fell to the ground, resting in the Spirit. Whitefield started the next month to preach to the Kingswood coal miners in the open fields. By March, 20,000 were attending. Whitefield invited Wesley to take over, and so in April Wesley began his famous open air preaching which continued for 50 years.

David Brainerd, missionary to the **North American Indians** saw a powerful visitation of God in October 1745. Whole communities were changed by the power of the Spirit. Crime and drunkenness dropped, idolatry was abandoned and marriages repaired.

In 1800 a powerful outpouring and revival touched **America**, especially the frontier territory of **Kentucky**. Thousands were converted. Many strange reactions accompanied the move of the Spirit then, including strong shaking and loud cries.

A man named Jeremiah Lanphier started holding noon prayer meetings in **New York** in September 1857. By October, it grew into a daily prayer meeting attended by many businessmen. By March 1858, newspapers carried front page reports of over 6,000 attending daily prayer meetings in **New York** and **Pittsburgh**. In

Washington five daily prayer meetings were held at five different times to accommodate the crowds. In May 1859, there was only about 800,000 people in New York, of which 50,000 were new converts. Charles Finney was preaching in those days. New England was profoundly changed by the revival and in several towns no unconverted adults could be found!

The Ulster revival of 1859 brought 100,000 converts into the churches of **Ireland**. It began with four men starting a weekly prayer meeting in a village school near Kells, in the month of September of 1857— the same date that prayer began in New York.

The awesome moves of God continued and increased in the 1900s around the world.

A few of these outpourings were:

The Welsh revival, 100,000 were converted in **Wales** during 1904-5.

Azusa Street in **Los Angeles** 1906, drew people from around the nation and overseas. There were awesome miracles and manifestations of the Spirit.

In the **Belgian Congo** in 1914 it was reported that the whole place was charged as if with an electric current. Men were falling, jumping, laughing, crying, singing, confessing, and some shaking terribly. This particular one can best be described as a spiritual tornado. People were literally flung to the floor or over the benches, yet no one was hurt. In prayer, the Spirit came down in mighty power sweeping the congregation — bodies trembled with the power — people were filled and as drunk with the Spirit.

In **Rwanda** in June 1936, the famous East African revival began and rapidly spread to the neighboring countries of **Burundi**, **Uganda**, and the **Congo** (now Zaire), then further.

Argentina in 1954, the largest stadium seating 110,000 was filled for weeks as 300,000 made commitments to Christ and hundreds were healed each night for three months.

God's power visited Asbury College in **Wilmore, Kentucky**, on February 3, 1970.

The Jesus Movement exploded among hippie and counter culture **youth in America** in the early seventies.

Nagaland, a state in the North East of **India**, began to experience revival in the 1960s and continued in revival. By the early 1980s it was estimated that 85% of the population had become Christians.

Many other outpourings and major moves of God have been reported in recent decades —far too many to mention here. Hundreds of thousands of people have been and are being converted — countless miracles of healing and deliverance from every evil work and darkness have been and are occurring.

In the decade of the 90s there was an increase in the major moves of God in the USA and around the world.

But we do not see these things on our evening news nor in many of our denominational reports.

A major Christian broadcasting network reported 6 million conversions in their work **worldwide** in 1990, which was more than the previous 30 years of results combined.

Revival swept **Cuba** in 1988. One church had 100,000 visitors in 6 months! A miraculous healing in one church led to nine days of meetings in which 1,200 people were saved. The pastors were imprisoned, but the revival continued. In another church where over 15,000 accepted Christ in three months. In 1990 a pastor whose congregation never exceeded 100 meeting once a week suddenly found himself conducting 12 services a day for 7,000 people.

In **East Germany** small prayer groups of ten to twelve persons started to pray for peace. By October 1989, 50,000 people were involved in Monday night prayer meetings. In 1990, when these praying people moved quietly into the streets, their numbers swelled to 300,000 and the wall came down.

Reports indicate that more **Muslims** have come to Christ in the past decade than in the previous thousand years.

An estimated 3.5 million people a year become Christian in **Latin America** now.

Evangelists continue to have massive healing evangelistic crusades in **Africa**, often with hundreds of thousands attending in the open air. In February, 1995, in Ethiopia, up to 115,000 attended meetings daily. In five days more than 100,000 made commitments to Christ and as many were filled with the Spirit and thousands received healing. Around 10 million a year are becoming Christians in Africa.

In **Benin (West Africa)**, on January 26 to 31, 1999, in a six day evangelistic campaign 640,000 people came to hear the Gospel, and some 200,000 called upon the Lord for salvation. Chains of demonic darkness and voodoo were broken. The glorious delivering power of God burst upon the multitudes. Many were pitifully pain-racked, afflicted, possessed and even insane. But when prayer was made, miracles took place just as in Biblical times - the blind saw, the deaf heard, the cripples walked, cancer victims were cured and mad people became sane. Mister Adoni was totally blind for 12 years. He was instantly healed and can now see.

An estimated 12 million a year are becoming Christian in **China** now with unprecedented moves of God's Spirit, healings, miracles, and visions of Christ.

Over **two billion people** have seen the Jesus film, the full-length movie based on the life of Christ. Showings have occurred in 230 nations and territories. Eight hundred twenty-one organizations use the evangelistic film, in addition to Campus Crusade for Christ International, which coordinates its international translation and distribution. **Eighty seven million** (87,000,000) people have indicated decisions to accept Jesus Christ as personal saviour.

In **Argentina** it is estimated that evangelical Christians tripled in five years to three million, about one tenth of the population. There was not room enough in the churches, some removed the seats so more people can be packed in. Thousands of people attended open-air meetings every night of the week in large cities where miracle healings were commonplace in every service.

There have been major outpourings in this decade, in the USA, numbers of conversions and renewed souls are beyond counting as powerful outpourings of God have brought revivals. New life has surged into hundreds of thousands of people, including many young people and children. Lives are reportedly being changed, addictions broken, relationships healed, documented miracles of healing are occurring, and worship has entered into a new level of living praise to God.

In **Toronto**, in 1994, 120 people had gathered for regular services when the power of God swept in and began to powerfully move upon the congregation. Since that time the outpouring has continued to this date with multitudes coming from around the world to be changed and to receive from God. Millions around the world have been touched by this renewal and who can count the conversions and radically changed lives?

In **Pensacola** on Fathers Day in 1995, the power of God swept into a denominational church. Hundreds of thousands have been converted as multitudes of people from all over the world have come to this powerful revival that continues to this day. Day after day hundreds ran to the alter in tears to give their lives to God. Long lines formed early in the morning outside the church for the 7:00 PM service that evening.

In **Smithton**, a Missouri farm town of 532 people, on March 24, 1996 at 6:12 PM, the power of God hit like a bolt of spiritual lightning in a small community church. For over four years, hundreds of people packed into the church for each of the five powerful services held each week. Over 250,000 people from every state in the USA and over 50 foreign countries have attended. No attempt is even made to keep count of the many conversions and multitudes of changed lives.

In **Baltimore**, on January 19, 1997, The power of God suddenly was poured out during the Sunday morning service. Revival began with powerful works of God and intense worship and praise. Again no attempt is made to keep up with the numbers of changed lives.

Like the first century Pharisees we can criticize these works and renounce them as something other than the works of God. Or we can sincerely pray and personally investigate some of these hot spots of spiritual outpouring in our day, as I have done and continue to do. It may not be wise to reject or accept on the basis of what the news media or someone else says. Until you have been to some of these places and experienced the powerful presence of God for yourself, no one can explain it to you. And once you have experienced the presence of God as the first century believers did and as multitudes are experiencing today you will know the truth.

Why not start now to earnestly pray for true renewal and revival to come to your church and your city? Prayer and willingness to change or two consistent prerequisites for true revival and real revival leads to the kingdom of God ruling in our lives and then our world.

Spiritual awakening of the kingdom of God through revival is the hope of the world.

The systems of the world cannot long continue to bear the burden of man's living apart from the ways of God. Nations have crumbled and will continue to do so under the weight of the cost of sinful pleasure and self indulgence. As the children of each generation without revival grow less able to make decisions that lead toward life and more unwilling to take responsibility for their own actions and lives, the cost increases. As the generations become more dependent, less productive, and unable to provide for themselves the cost becomes unbearable to governments and a strain on all the systems of the planet.

Thank God for spiritual awakening -- for with it comes awakening of reality thinking by God's people. Men's minds are being freed and the flow of godly wisdom is returning to cause mankind to find his way to real life and away from the seducing trickery of self indulgence and carnal pleasure seeking. People set free by the power of God in revival become God seekers who seek to know Him and to walk in obedience to His ways. Once freed from carnal pleasure seeking and self indulgence, the people begin to loose their bent toward violence. Without their appetites for violence and carnal pleasure, people become free to love and serve one another as they love and serve God with their whole hearts.

REVIVAL IS NOT OPTIONAL

And compared to the alternative it is not too costly. The alternative to not having revival in our world is unthinkable. The cost is beyond compare. To count the stars of heaven would be easier than counting the total cost of not having revival in our world. No amount of cost we pay for revival, either individually, or collectively world wide is too much. Any amount of cost of our lives and effort is worth paying for world revival.

God is pouring out His Spirit in this time and the potential for world wide revival is a reality in this day and the days just ahead. The time for religious debate and walls of separation between real life and God's people is past. Revival is destroying separations and will eventually destroy the separation of God and governments of many nations of the world.

National governments and ungodly ruling institutions are now feeling threatened by the reality of the kingdom of God coming forth in the World. They will be changed or brought down by the power and presence of God as revival and reformation sweeps the land. As God continues to pour out His Spirit and His people respond with unrestrained praise and worship and gather themselves unto Him in intimate prayer, revival is changing our world. No price is too great in response to the One who gave His life on the cross to become the resurrected Christ indwelling His people bringing revival to the world.

BASILEIA LETTER

Number 26

Innocence In The Kingdom of God

*Jesus said, I am sending you out like sheep among wolves. Therefore be as shrewd as snakes and as **innocent** as doves.* Mat 10:16 NIV

In this first century of the new millennium the Body of Christ is awakening to the reality of innocence. It seems we may have sought to be as wise as a serpent or shrewd as a snake and missed the Lord's instruction to be **innocent, harmless,** and **pure**.

Pastor Steve Gray of the Smithton Outpouring / World Revival Church said something that touched me deeply. He said, "Jesus is more real to me today than ever. As He has come nearer and nearer and I have had an even better glimpse of Him. **I have been shocked — not by His fire and power but by His innocence — a pure and innocent lamb that has never sinned — completely pure and innocent.**"

At the core of our Lord's matchless glory, His fire, and His power, is **His heart of innocence** -- completely and totally pure -- not even a hint of uncleanness nor a speck of disobedience to the Father. **He is the completely blameless and harmless innocent lamb of God.** In this time of outpouring, as His presence is more known to us and we become more intimate with Him, we are glimpsing more of His true character.

*Heb 7:26 NIV: Such a high priest meets our need--**one who is holy, blameless, pure, set apart from sinners, exalted above the heavens.***

Innocence In The Kingdom of God

> We are beginning to grasp an understanding of the relationship between utter innocence and unlimited power.

The very center of His matchless glory, power, and authority is His absolute perfect innocence and purity. As only a perfect gem without inner impurity or flaw can perfectly flow the pure light without distortion, only perfect absolute innocence can flow the pure light and power of God. Any impurity or flaw would produce distortion and become harmful when the light and power of God is increased.

We desire to be like Him to be in the presence of His glory and to flow His unlimited wisdom and power bringing healing, restoration, renewal, reformation and revival to the world. But we are not like Him and cannot do these things because we are not innocent like him. Our man focused preaching and lukewarm lifestyles mixed with cares of this life and desire for things of the world are not innocent like him. Our zealousness to protect and defend our narrow view of the very limited doctrines and religious forms we cherish, causes us to become harmful and we are not innocent. Doctrinal wars and debate over form do not flow from a heart of utter innocence. Striving against brothers, back biting and gossiping are not from a heart of innocence and are not harmless and pure. Even our best is often not innocent like Him.

Phil 2:14-15 NIV: **Do everything without complaining or arguing, so that you may become blameless and pure, children of God without fault in a crooked and depraved generation, in which you shine like stars in the universe.**

While church members debate and actually get into fist fights in the church over whether to use hymn books or an overhead projector, and while churches split over selecting the color of the new carpet and other such foolish strife, the world starves for the reality of God to show forth the pure and innocent heart of Christ.

While political church leadership attempts to cover its impurities and defend itself and friends and attacks others to protect a position of power over people, the prisoners of the pew starve and die for lack of real food from God. They are given only fake food. That plastic stuff that looks so real in the restaurant window but has no nutritional value and cannot really be eaten.

As we experience His innocence, our pride and self strength melts and our hearts are broken because of the impurity and defilement of our lives contaminated by self living and bad religious training. His glorious presence comes down as we give ourselves to Him in corporate praise, deep adoration of worship and focused prayer. Entering intimacy of His presence begins to reveal His innocence and our hearts are broken by the depth of his purity and innocence. Our lives are exposed to us and we feel as if we have walked into the perfect palace of purity in our dirty work clothes. We begin to understand the parable of the guest entering the wedding feast without a proper wedding garment.

Our hearts weep and tears flow as we see the innocence of our husband and recognize the uncleanness and unfitness of our lives to become the Bride and enter into further intimacy with the innocence of God Himself. Our bodies crumple to the floor and we cannot even open our eyes as our inner parts convulse with sorrow at our inability to enter into the fullness of intimacy with Him. In this deep repentance we feel great changes occurring as things are ripped out of our innermost being leaving gaping holes to be filled with His love and innocent purity.

Eventually we arise from the floor to lift our hands and hearts to Him in wonderful adoration from renewed hearts. Joy burst into our souls as we realize we are more like Him now than we were moments ago. The process continues as we are becoming the prepared Bride for the innocent Lamb the roaring Lion of God.

We have no pride or fear and will no longer remain in the pew as prisoners of religion. Revolution is inevitable as we enter into the glorious reality of the presence of God Himself and all tolerance for religions bondage of traditions and man centered doctrines leaves us. There is great love for God and His people, especially those remaining in the bondage of religious political systems. But there is no loyalty to the systems which may have retained a facsimile of the truth but have brought great perversion and distortion to the truth of the pure innocent Christ and His potential Bride.

Power and wisdom are directly and proportionately related to innocence.

We may have read many times *Mat 10:16 NIV, I am sending you out like sheep among wolves. Therefore be as shrewd as snakes and as **innocent** as doves.* Or in the KJV, *Behold, I send you forth as sheep in the midst of wolves: be ye therefore wise as serpents, and harmless as doves.* I have always noticed the contrast of being as wise or shrewd as a snake and as innocent or harmless as a dove and never before understood the relationship of these things.

Power and wisdom of God come to the innocent.

The harmless and innocent ones will hear and receive wisdom and revelation to function powerfully (shrewdly) in this perverse world. Only the innocent and harmless can be trusted with the great secrets of power and strategy from God. Only the innocent sheep can have the shrewd wisdom to deal with the wolves of this world and not become contaminated by the ways of the wicked.

The Body of Christ is now beginning to awaken to the potential power of purity. Our innocence will become the source of power to fuel the great revolution bringing an end to man centered and devil enhanced religious systems of the world.

Now is the time to seek Him with our whole heart and to lay down quickly those things He brings to our attention. We must enter collectively in the power of all in unity corporately to experience the glorious presence of God that changes us from glory to glory. We are becoming more like Him and He shall roar out of Zion in the unlimited power of innocence. The world is waiting and groaning for you and me and an army of young people to become innocent and harmless that we may be wise and shrewd -- the innocent army of God bringing a revolution of reformation establishing the kingdom of God on earth as it is in heaven.

From positional righteousness to real purity of innocence.

My heart was broken because of my sinful condition when as a young man of twenty one I encountered the saving grace of our Lord Jesus. My heart's desire was to be different, to be like Him and to be pleasing in His sight. Some things about me did change very quickly. I felt very bad every time a curse word leaked out of my mouth from my not yet renewed mind and soon I was mostly free of that profane habit. Yet many other things within and about me were not like Him.

My concerns about my debauchery were greatly eased by theological teachings of positional righteousness. Basically I was taught that my depravity was normal and that my disgraceful unholy inner life was covered by the blood of Jesus. Everyone was a sinner and now I was a saved sinner and would be in heaven because of what Jesus had done on the cross for me. My position was that of now being seated at the right hand of God with Christ, redeemed by the blood. When God looked at me He did not see my sinfulness but the righteousness of Christ. Certainly, I was to try to do my best but I could never expect to overcome sin in this life because of my sin nature. We all are sinners only some are saved sinners and some are lost sinners.

According to this teaching I was positionally innocent before God because Jesus had died for me and my sins past, present, and future were under the blood of Jesus. Because I believed in Jesus as the Son of God and had received Him as saviour I was secure and could not be plucked from His hand. Yet, my experience continued to be a roller coaster type of spiritual ups and sinful downs. Although I sought diligently to hide my lust and to overcome sinful habits and addictions my life was a battle of bitter frustration. Zealousness characterized my life. I fought hard against my own inner impurities and was severely harsh against sin in others.

I taught Sunday School, became an elder in the church, attended Bible College, began preaching, witnessed in the streets, and visited for the church. Yet, in all my zealousness, impurities remained within my own heart. I was not innocent and harmless as a dove and often wondered how and why most everyone close to me seemed to get hurt or offended by me. The intent of my heart was pure but it is from the abundance of the heart that the life speaks. (Luke 6:45)

Like many others around the world, My soul cried out, **"there must be more"**.

The "more" has now come. The outpouring of the Spirit has brought power from God to change our inner being to eradicate our sinful ways and fill us with His purity and power. No longer must we suffer in frustration as sin takes its toll upon the strength and glory of God within our souls. Freedom is upon us as the spiritual outpouring of God is bringing revival to our souls and reformation to the blessed Body of Christ who is becoming His purified Bride. No longer must we attempt to replace our lack of spiritual power with soulish zealousness. (Rom 10:2-3)

We can now be filled with the power of His presence cleansing our hearts and destroying our desire for the old ways. No longer are we focused upon our own lives and filled with needs. His love flowing in and through us is making us innocent and harmless. His presence has so filled us that we have no frustrating needs but are filled with abundant life to flow to others.

No longer must we devise doctrines to make room for our sinful hearts. Christ is not just a covering for our sin filled heart. Now, when God looks at us He can look directly into a pure heart filled with the innocence and glory of Christ Himself. The reality of God has come and the shadows are passing away.

The army of God is being formed. Pure hearts of ordinary believers have become the temple of God on earth and the attributes of God are becoming a reality in the innocent and harmless people of God's army. Truly nothing is impossible as pure hearts are filled with great faith and ability to know God and discern His will. Clearly receiving His instruction and having the faith to act upon it provides unlimited power to accomplish the will of God on earth as it is in heaven.

The outpouring of God coming forth in spots around the world in this time is not just for the purpose of our having a Holy Ghost party. The joy of the Lord is real and the excitement of miracles and manifestations along with the awesome praise and worship music are indeed producing many occasions of gloriously wonderful gatherings. The many testimonies of miracles and healing of bodies and lives is exciting. The stories told by those being saved and delivered as well as those returning to the Lord after straying away are uplifting. All of this is joyful and is indeed a part of the purpose for the great outpouring of God in the world today. But, if it does not lead to inner purity and innocence, God's purpose is not fulfilled. If we can experience God and His blessings and still leave the gathering to return to our old thought patterns and our old ways of doing and being, God's purpose is not yet fulfilled. If our lifestyle continues to be mixed with the spirit of the world, we are missing the purpose of God.

This is a new day for the church. The church that taught us self improvement, self love, prosperity for the sake of our blessing and tolerance for our sinful lifestyles is now over. The twelve o'clock whistle has blown, the final amen has been said and the entire church has gone to lunch. We must come to the realization that church as usual is over and is not coming back. Yes, many will hang on to the man centered gospel and the old ways of the church until they themselves pass away in the wilderness. Many will continue to carry forth the empty traditions of the past until they breathe their last natural breath. They have already breathed their last spiritual breath and are only waiting to die in their wilderness experience while seeking to prevent others from entering the promised land.

These are our spiritual mothers and fathers and there is a reality of honor for them. Yet, we must hate their ways and the ungodly part of the things they have taught us and demanded that we continue. Is this a part of what Jesus meant when He said in Luke 14:26 that we could not be His disciple if we did not hate our father and mother? We know that we are not to hate the church or our parents. But we must hate what they are saying to us that prevents us from going on with Jesus and being a part of what He is doing in this day. We must hate the encouragement to continue in our mixed ways of inner impurity and tolerance for sin. We must hate the thing that continues to tell us that we are doing well when inside we are filled with death and are not concerned about living a truly consecrated life unto the Lord.

Just as long as we are reasonably healthy and doing well financially we tend to be satisfied and don't really mind our immoral lifestyles and lack of the true presence of God in our midst. Much of the church today is yet saying, as long as we have really nice cars, the finest church buildings ever, time for the golf course, and plenty of entertainment why rock the boat. Why start a revolution bringing reformation and revival.

Only when the true presence of God shows up and begins to expose the bankrupt spiritual condition of the powerless church does it become obvious that something is terribly wrong. The lukewarm half hearted people who are mixed with the ways of the world will either be changed or deny the work of God and flee from His presence.

BASILEIA LETTER

Number 27

Pain & Suffering
In the Kingdom of God

Jesus said, *"O My Father, if it is possible, let this cup pass from Me; nevertheless, not as I will, but as You will.", Mat 26:39.*

Heb 12:2a: Looking unto Jesus, the author and finisher of our faith, who for the joy that was set before Him **endured the cross, despising the shame.**

1 Pet 2:20-21: For what credit is it if, when you are beaten for your faults, you take it patiently? **But when you do good and suffer,** *if you take it patiently, this is commendable before God. For to this you were called, because* **Christ also suffered for us, leaving us an example, that you should follow His steps.**

In my mind I can still hear the voice of President Franklin D. Rosevelt as he spoke the declaration of war in December of 1941. World War II was officially declared that night as my father, mother, my siblings, and I gathered in somber silence around the radio. In his deep, serious, and strong but mellow voice he spoke these words, **"I hate war. --- My wife Elenor hates war. --- We all hate war."** He went on to speak of the evil attacks against our nation and that because of evil, war was necessary. He then sought to encourage the nation to fight. He encouraged the men to fight for the lives and futures of their children and their families. He encouraged the families to sacrifice and give all they could to help their husbands, fathers, and sons that were going into mortal combat to stop the enemy.

This sleepy nation was suddenly awakened. The jolt of devastating attack had shaken us to the core and instantly the focus of the entire nation was on fighting and winning the war. We were so far behind in preparation and such a devastating blow had been dealt to our navy that we were not sure who would win the war. In the days, months, and years ahead the enemy advanced rapidly and we continued to retreat on all fronts with heavy casualties. Almost every person in the USA was affected personally by the pain and suffering of the war. Though we cried a lot, our focus was never on the fear or the pain but on winning the war and the hope of victory. Hundreds of thousands of young men laid down the tools of their trade and picked up a rifle with a bayonet fixed on it and became fighting men. They endured the pain and suffering of battle and died trying to stop the enemy's advance.

Pain is never a gift from God except as an indicator of disorder. It is not His desire for mankind. Yet, because of the evil of man, pain and suffering are very real. Those who will live as Christ in the world will be partakers of His pain and suffering.

2 Tim 3:12-13: ***Yes, and all who desire to live godly in Christ Jesus will suffer persecution.***

Jesus came to earth and accepted the cup of suffering for the joy of the glory of the kingdom of God. Had there been no evil in the world, Jesus would not have endured pain and suffering. If there were no need in the church and no evil in our world today, we would not be compelled to endure pain and suffering today.

Col 1:24 I now rejoice in my sufferings for you, and fill up in my flesh what is lacking in the afflictions of Christ, for the sake of His body, which is the church.

In the days of this writing we are living in a time of great mercy of God. A time in which the outpouring of the Spirit of God is bringing renewal and revival to many spots in the world. Renewal is bringing great blessing and joyful presence of God and even something called by some a "Holy Ghost party", so called because of the great joy the presence of God brings. There is great praise and worship expressed in music, dance, shouts of rejoicing as well as times of quite intimate communion with God. Physical manifestations of the Spirit and miracles are not uncommon.

Many of these revived and rejoicing believers were once a part of other churches and religious systems. Some have given much of their lives and resources to their previous church fellowships and denominations only to find that they were unwelcome and unwanted when the powerful presence of God swept over them. Often evil reports and false accusations are brought to slander those who are revived by the Spirit of God. Family members sometimes reject them causing painful splits within families which sometimes brings financial losses and loss of social position. In some parts of the world believers are beaten, imprisoned, taken into slavery, and sometimes martyred because of their love for Jesus.

There have been those of the church in the past who have given their all and sought to serve God with their whole heart and to reach the world. They were the exceptions, the ones who were different, the revivalist, the missionaries, the saints who gave up secular life to serve to the best of their ability with their whole heart. Often spending their entire lives and seeing very little fruit in a spiritually sleeping world. Here and their a great awakening would occur only to be eventually smothered by the religious church of the past and drowned with tradition and debate over form and strife among denominations.

In the passing church age, religion has lulled its followers to sleep with lullabies of peace and doctrines of false security brought forth by religious demons.

1 Tim 4:1 Now the Spirit expressly says that in latter times some will depart from the faith, **giving heed to deceiving spirits and doctrines of demons.**

Jer 6:14 They have also healed the hurt of My people slightly, **Saying, 'Peace, peace!' When there is no peace.**

Most of the religious world did not even know that a spiritual war was going on and that the enemy was subversively infiltrating the religious and secular world with corrupt beliefs that robbed believers of the joyful and powerful presence of God which would have brought forth His kingdom in the earth.

For the most part, the church slept and did not even show up for the war and has lost by default.

The rule of the earth has been given over to the enemy without even a fight.

The lives and souls of multitudes of men women and children across the world have been lost. Our families are destroyed. Our children are spiritually raped and murdered and robbed of all potential power in the kingdom of God while we are comfortable with our favorite TV shows of filth and violence and our beliefs of liberal self gratification, and while the church fights over doctrines and debates manifestations.

Though there were many victories, **the church of the past has failed** to conquer the enemy and bring forth the kingdom of God. We cannot blame the devil whom Jesus has defeated. We cannot blame the lost and heathen world. They knew nothing and had no potential without the church becoming powerful to reach them. We must put the blame where it belongs, on ourselves. **Believers who have been deceived and have swallowed a camel of false doctrine and strained at gnats of truth.** Believers who considered ourselves, our lives, our comfort, and our religion above the kingdom of God. Believers who did not even know there was a kingdom of God here and now. A sick and deadly religious group of half hearted lukewarm powerless believers consumed with our own controversies and strife over useless wrangling over doctrines of baptisms and ordinances of which we knew nothing of the reality of the life these things proclaimed.

Today much of the sleeping church only wakes up to fight against the true move of God coming forth in powerful revivals around the world. They are harsh in defending their sacred doctrines and do not know that they are defending mixtures of truth and doctrines of demons and religious traditions of men. The church has been so trained in inner combat and to ignore the enemy who has taken them captive, that even those being set free tend to turn their guns upon each other and from habit and training they debate the different streams of revival and moves of God rather than joining together to destroy the enemy and bringing forth the kingdom of God.

The hearts and minds of men, women, and children are being changed by the powerful presence of God coming forth in our world today. The great transition from dead religion to the reality of the outpouring of the presence and power of God is bringing great change into our world. No longer are we the center of the gospel. No longer are we the center of our own world. Christ Jesus is receiving His rightful place as king of our lives and eventually king over all the kingdoms of our world. There is no more place for lukewarm and half hearted Christianity. The presence of God is consuming His people like a consuming fire as revival sweeps our hearts.

Heb 12:28 -29: Therefore, since we are receiving a kingdom which cannot be shaken, let us have grace, by which we may serve God acceptably with reverence and godly fear.
For our God is a consuming fire.

The dying religious churches must give up their prideful position of believing they know everything and have all there is of God and bow their lives and beliefs before God. They must cry out for His mercy to cover them while there is yet mercy in this time of transition. This time of mercy will not last forever and the days of judgment will come upon the church. (1 Pet 4:17) She will be judged because of her lack of repentance from deception, spiritual darkness and blindness, which led her to oppose the move of God upon the earth today. While she thought she was the elite and chosen of God, rich in spiritual knowledge, she is a doomed and dying generation that must repent or die in the wilderness. Thinking herself to be rich she became naked and poor and now is in danger of being left behind as the mighty move of God upon the earth is bringing transition from the man centered church age to the God centered kingdom of God age. Now is the time for wise men to repent and pay the price to make the great changes necessary to get out of lukewarm religion and into the powerful presence and flow of God.

*Rev 3:16-19; "So then, **because you are lukewarm, and neither cold nor hot, I will vomit you out of My mouth. "Because you say, 'I am rich, have become wealthy, and have need of nothing'; and do not know that you are wretched, miserable, poor,*** *blind, and naked; "I counsel you to buy from Me gold refined in the fire, that you may be rich; and white garments, that you may be clothed, that the shame of your nakedness may not be revealed; and anoint your eyes with eye salve, that you may see. "As many as I love, I rebuke and chasten.* ***Therefore be zealous and repent.***

The true people of God of today will never back down, never turn back and never quit. The revivals and the move of God today will not be smothered by religion or stopped by debate and strife. The people will not be stopped by suffering, pain, or death. This move of God will take the earth as young people across the world come to know the true love of God and become pure in their hearts to carry the cross of Christ into glorious blazing resurrection life.

The glory of God is now coming forth on the earth in His sons and daughters.

Christ Jesus is now being valued above riches, knowledge, worldly esteem, marriage and family and yes, even life itself. The most important thing to the pure hearted sons and daughters of God is not their own life, not even the lives of their children as deeply important as these things are, the most important thing is Jesus and his presence with us and His glory revealed.

A generation of people are coming forth upon the earth with a new value system. One that does not ignore the things of natural life but one that values God so far above all else that there is no close second. **To the rest of the world and to the devil and his demons this is a most frightening thing.** Nothing can be used to entice or divert the arising army of God. There is no place for the world or the devil to get their hooks into the self abandoned and empowered children of God.

We are entering the time for which the servants of God have waited throughout history. The time of redemption on a scale never before seen and that will never be seen again. A time when absolutely nothing is impossible to those who truly believe. A time that will see the destruction of the past religious world and the evil secular world which will not repent. The unrepentant will cry out for the mountains and the rocks to fall on them and hide them from the face of the completely innocent glorious all powerful God. The more the enemy and religion kills, the more children will be raised up by the mighty hand of God. The great harvest of the earth has begun in the pure hearted children of God who no longer count their lives as precious to themselves and value Christ Jesus above all else.

This is spiritual warfare in its total reality. This war will be won in the presence and power of almighty God himself coming in the outpouring of His Spirit bringing a pouring out of the Spirit of God through His people. It will be won in praise, worship, dancing, rejoicing before the Lord, and intimate oneness with Jesus. It is the reality of "Christ in you the hope of glory." In revival today Christ Jesus is returning to earth in His people to establish His kingdom and to rule and reign with His saints. The devil and the religions of the world cannot stop the very presence of God in His people walking upon the earth in the power of Christ doing all the works that Jesus did and more. (John 14:12)

This is not the time for human effort to attempt to do the works of the church. **Church growth is not the issue. The issue for the religious church is church destruction.** The old must come down to make place for the new. The only question is, will the people who have sought God in the religious man centered systems, turn and repent and seek Him with their whole hearts? Or will they wait to be torn down and destroyed by the work of the enemy who has seduced and deceived them? Will they seek deliverance and come out of the open prison door and receive sight for their spiritual blindness as many others already have?

Jesus is today proclaiming the opening of the prison for those who are bound (in religion), those who mourn in Zion (the church). The sons of God are anointed of the Lord to proclaim good tidings to those who may have thought they were rich but are really spiritually poor, blind, and in bondage to a mixture of truth and deception.

*Isa 61:1-3: "The Spirit of the Lord GOD is upon Me, Because the LORD has anointed Me To preach good tidings to the **poor**; He has sent Me to heal the brokenhearted, To proclaim liberty to the captives, **And the opening of the prison to those who are bound**; To proclaim the acceptable year of the LORD, And the day of vengeance of our God; **To comfort all who mourn, To console those who mourn in Zion,** To give them beauty for ashes, The oil of joy for mourning, The garment of praise for the spirit of heaviness; That they may be called trees of righteousness, The planting of the LORD, that He may be glorified."*

Wake up people of God! This is for you! The bondages of religious doctrines and false security brought forth in the darkness of past religious bondage can no longer hold you. The religious prison doors are open. There is comfort and beauty for you. There is power, joy and praise in the presence and glory of the Lord waiting for you now. Come out from among the unclean religious systems and God will be a Father to you. You will find life in His presence and experience His love in a greater way than ever before.

*2 Cor 6:17 - 7:4: **Therefore "Come out from among them And be separate, says the Lord. Do not touch what is unclean, And I will receive you." "I will be a Father to you, And you shall be My sons and daughters, Says the LORD Almighty."***

*Therefore, having these promises, beloved, let us cleanse ourselves from all filthiness of the flesh **and spirit**, perfecting holiness in the fear of God. Open your hearts to us. We have wronged no one, we have corrupted no one, we have cheated no one. I do not say this to condemn; for I have said before that you are in our hearts, to die together and to live together. Great is my boldness of speech toward you, great is my boasting on your behalf. **I am filled with comfort. I am exceedingly joyful in all our tribulation.***

BASILEIA LETTER

Number 28
Victory In the Kingdom of God

"Basileia Letter" is changing. As we enter the time of great harvest of the earth there are many changes to come forth. To be effective in turbulent times we must be quick to change and to flow with what God is doing. "Basileia Letters" and the books "Overcoming Life On A Small Planet" and "The Seventh Millennium" are written for the purpose of teaching some of the fundamentals of the kingdom of God and helping to bring people through the process of reformation from man centered church to God centered kingdom of God living on earth.

This work has just begun. There are relatively few people who have truly grasped the gospel of the kingdom and the potential that lies within the hearts of believers to rule and reign with Christ now in every area of life and government. Even the most powerful moves of revival and reformation in the world today have only a start of the revelation of the potential of the glory of Christ in man ruling and reigning in the world. Therefore the work of these books and letters shall go on for many years and perhaps centuries to come as one by one believers find the truth of the kingdom of God now.

These and other works by other men of God are the beginnings of kingdom understanding. It had to start with those who had nothing to loose. The established church and ministry leaders cannot be first in bringing forth the fresh revelation of kingdom. They have to much to loose by the rejection of those believers who are yet unable to change and flow in the new stream of restored revelation. God in his mercy temporarily withholds the enlightenment of leaders of revival and reformation movements to the fullness of the gospel of the kingdom now to prevent confusion of the troops who are required to bring about the harvest that is at hand. New and fresh wine can be too much of a taste change for the survival of unity in the ranks of the army of harvesters in our world.

Therefore, God has chosen to gradually re introduce the gospel of the kingdom through non threatening methods and non threatening men. He has chosen to use unknown and in many cases older men of God who have largely finished their season of gathering and therefore no longer need respect as significant or popular leaders. A base of believers who are receiving the gospel of the kingdom are coming forth and the kingdom is coming up like grass covering a field and not like great trees. Intermingled with the grass of the field are the tiny new trees that will eventually grow to become the great trees of future kingdom of God leaders.

Prophets Point The Way

Prophets are not designed to be great gatherers, but plowers that destroy the old, and planters of the new kingdom seed that covers the fields as grass and one day shall grow the trees of the future. God is raising up young prophets with strong words of the gospel of the kingdom. And of course the enemy is raising up false kingdom prophets who plant seeds of a kingdom that looks like the kingdom of God but is really tares.

"Basileia Letters" will, in the near future, all be bound in book form and along with Overcoming Life and Seventh Millennium will continue to be made available to the body of Christ. These works can be helpful in discerning the true and false prophets of kingdom as well as helping to plant and grow the seeds of the kingdom of God into the kingdom lifestyle in our world. These books can be requested and Basileia Letters downloaded from our web site: http://www.basileiapublishing.com/

> In the kingdom of God, Victory is God ruling over all the kingdoms of earth through His people, not just ruling in the church or the individual.

Many believers are yet looking to the bodily return of Jesus to bring victory. Until the masses realize that Jesus has already done everything he will ever do to destroy the kingdoms of the enemy without our participation, the kingdoms of this earth cannot become the kingdoms of our God. Until believers understand that the ball is in our court, that we are empowered by God to destroy the work of the enemy and establish the rule of God in the earth, it cannot yet be done. The kingdom of God is not waiting for God to make another move. It is waiting on mankind to realize and move into what God has already provided through Christ Jesus. **The honor of God must be restored on earth by mankind.** Man dishonored God in the Garden of Eden and surrendered the kingdoms of this world to the enemy and until the kingdoms are returned to our God He is dishonored on earth.

Until this final victory is achieved the Basileia Letters and other books we have mentioned will not have finished their work. The fulfillment of my life and the lives of all the men of God who have come and gone before me and have seen the kingdom of God yet afar off cannot be complete until the day the kingdoms of this earth become the kingdoms of our God. Our mission must be completed in future generations if this generation will not come to the reality of giving our lives to restore honor to God in recapturing the kingdoms of this world. He has given us His great power within us and is now working with us from heaven. Jesus must remain bodily in heaven while He battles for earth in His Bride -- His Body on earth.

The fullness of victory remains incomplete -- not because of God or anything He needs to do -- but because of man and what he chooses to believe. Mankind does not want to accept the responsibility which he ultimately cannot escape. He wants victory to completely rest in God and have nothing to do with himself. The enlightenment of the truth that God will do nothing further to redeem the kingdoms of earth without man's willing participation is hard for man to accept. Men love darkness which covers their lack of willingness to die to self and honor God by redeeming the kingdoms of earth with the awesome power of God available through a willing participant.

To cover his lack man has invented doctrines of perversions of God's grace. God's grace gifts of power are to overcome the world and destroy the work of the enemy for the purpose of redeeming the kingdoms of this world for our God and restoring honor unto His name. God's grace is not a whitewash covering for man's sin of non participation and self centered living which only honor the devil and not God. God's grace is the unmerited favor of the power of God given to believers to redeem the kingdoms of the world. Christ Jesus has done everything to redeem the kingdom and is restoring honor to the Father by bringing righteous living and obedience forth in the world through His body on earth, the purified Bride church.

> For now, our victory is the redemption
> of His kingdom within the individual
> rather than full corporate kingdom.

While the purified Bride church groups are growing and the grass of the fields is coming forth and the kingdom is waiting for believers to believe, we are blessed with personal victory and increasing victory in groups. In spots around the world the kingdom of God is coming forth in groups as revival fires continue to spread. Individually and in some groups we are restoring honor to God and recapturing portions of the kingdoms of this world as the work of the enemy is being destroyed and righteousness established in the earth.

The important thing is that we each finish our part. That we remain faithful to the end to carry out all God has put within our hands to do and to be. It is important that we complete the portion of destroying the kingdom of darkness and establishing the kingdom of our God that we are gifted to do during our time on earth. It is important that we leave a legacy for the future generations that have a fresh chance to take back the kingdoms of earth and restore honor to our God. Each generation has the opportunity to begin where the previous one finished. Our greatest hope is to hear those words, "well done good and faithful servant" and to know we have had a part in restoring His honor and bringing His kingdom forth on earth.

The great harvest has begun. Millions are gathering to hear the salvation message and experience the presence and power of God flowing through His servants. Praise, worship, strong corporate prayer and righteous living is restoring honor to our God. The great army is being assembled as multitudes are finding personal redemption in God and giving their lives to serve Him. These masses of mostly young believers must eventually hear and receive the gospel of the kingdom and become soldiers carrying the gospel of the kingdom to all the world. The political world, financial world, the world of education and every facet of our world will all be transformed as the mass of believers each do their part in conducting the business of the world.

The natural course of judgmental destruction set in motion by mankind living apart from God's ways for centuries will bring great adjustments in the world toward the kingdom of God in the future. For now in this time of mercy and visitation of the presence of God we must fan the fires of revival and seek to bring forth the glorious presence of God leading toward the great world harvest.

Our future periodical publications at Basileia Publishing will reflect that change. Our thought at this time is to publish a shorter communication called "Doxa Dispatch". Doxa is the New Testament Greek word for glory. This communication will remain true to the gospel of the kingdom and seek to spread the fire of His glory and fan the fires of revival moving toward the great harvest. This will be your last "Basileia Letter." May we suggest that you reread them in the books, "Basileia Letters Volume 1 & 2". Look for kingdom wisdom in the new shorter Basileia publication "Doxa Dispatch" coming soon.

~~~~~~

Author's Note

Wherefore I will not be negligent to put you always in remembrance of these things, though ye know them, and be established in the present truth.

Yea, I think it meet, as long as I am in this tabernacle, to stir you up by putting you in remembrance; Knowing that shortly I must put off this my tabernacle, even as our Lord Jesus Christ hath shown me.

Moreover I will endeavour that ye may be able after my decease to have these things always in remembrance.

For we have not followed cunningly devised fables, when we made known unto you the power and presence of our Lord Jesus Christ, but are eyewitnesses of his majesty, 2 Pet 1:12-16.

In His love,
Brother Ron